# WHOL-I-NESS

## HOLY, WHOLLY, HOLEY

### Seven Dimensions of a Whole Person

General Editor
LYMAN COLEMAN

Managing Editor
DENISE BELTZNER

Assistant Editors
DOUGLAS LABUDDE
KEITH MADSEN
STEPHEN SHEELY

Cover Art
CHRISTOPHER WERNER

Cover Design
ERIKA TIEPEL

Layout Production
FRONTLINE GROUP

Serendipity House/Box 1012/Littleton, CO 80160    1-800-525-9563
95 96 97 98 99 /CH/ 6 5 4 3 2 1

**ACKNOWLEDGMENTS**

To Zondervan Bible Publishers
for permission to use
the NIV text,
*The Holy Bible, New International Version*
©1973, 1978, 1984 by International Bible Society.
Used by permission of Zondervan Bible Publishers

# INSTRUCTIONS FOR GROUP LEADER

**PURPOSE:** **What is this course all about?** To discover what it means to be a whole person in every area of your life while in a supportive group.

**SEEKERS/ STRUGGLERS:** **Who is this course designed for?** Two kinds of people: (a) Seekers who do not know where they are with God but are open to finding out, and (b) Strugglers who are committed to Jesus Christ, but want to grow in their faith.

**NEW PEOPLE:** **Does this mean I can invite my non-church friends?** Absolutely. In fact, this would be a good place for people on their way back to God to start.

**STUDY:** **What are we going to study?** Seven dimensions of a whole person (see inside front cover) and what the Bible has to say about each of them.

**FIRST SESSION:** **What do we do at the meetings?** In the first session, you get acquainted and decide on the Ground Rules for your group. In sessions two through seven, you have two Options for Bible study.

**TWO OPTIONS:** **What are the two options?** OPTION ONE—This study is best for newly-formed groups or groups that are unfamiliar with small group Bible study. This option primarily contains multiple-choice questions, with no "right or wrong" answers.

OPTION TWO—This study is best for groups who have had previous small group Bible studies and want to dig deeper into the Scriptures. Option Two questions are deeper—and the Scripture is a teaching passage.

**CHOOSING AN OPTION:** **Which option of Bible study do you recommend?** The OPTION ONE study is best for newly-formed groups, groups that are unfamiliar with small group Bible study, or groups that are only meeting for an hour. The OPTION TWO study is best for deeper Bible study groups, or groups which meet for more than an hour.

**CHOOSING BOTH OPTIONS:** **Can we choose both options?** If your group meets for 90 to 120 minutes, you can choose to do both studies at the same time. Or you can spend two weeks on a unit—OPTION ONE the first week and OPTION TWO the next. Or you can do one of the options in the meeting and the other option for homework.

**SMALL GROUP:** **What is different about this course?** It is written for a small group to do together.

**OUP BUILDING:** **What is the purpose behind your approach to Bible study?** To give everyone a chance to share their own "spiritual story," and to bond as a group. This is often referred to as "koinonia."

**KOINONIA:** **What is koinonia and why is it a part of these studies?** Koinonia means "fellowship." It is an important part of these sessions, because as a group gets to know one another, they are more willing to share their needs and care for one another.

**BIBLE KNOWLEDGE:** **What if I don't know much about the Bible?** No problem. Option One is based on a Bible story that stands on its own—to discuss as though you were hearing it for the first time. Option Two comes with Comments —to keep you up to speed.

**COMMENTS:** **What is the purpose of the Comments?** To help you understand the context of the Bible passage.

**LEADERSHIP:** **Who leads the meetings?** Ideally, there should be three people: (a) trained leader, (b) apprentice or co-leader, and (c) host. Having an apprentice-in-training in the group, you have a built-in system for multiplying the group if it gets too large. In fact, this is one of the goals of the group—to give "birth" to a new group in time.

**RULES:** **What are the ground rules for the group?**

PRIORITY: While you are in the course, you give the group meetings priority.

PARTICIPATION: Everyone participates and no one dominates.

RESPECT: Everyone is given the right to their own opinion, and "dumb questions" are encouraged and respected.

CONFIDENTIALITY: Anything that is said in the meeting is never repeated outside the meeting.

EMPTY CHAIR: The group stays open to new people at every meeting as long as they understand the ground rules.

SUPPORT: Permission is given to call upon each other in time of need at any time.

CONTINUING: What happens to the group after finishing this course? The group is free to disband or continue to another course. (See pages 63–64 for making a Covenant and continuing together as a group.)

FOUR THINGS YOU NEED TO KNOW ABOUT
# Beginning a Small Group

**1. PURPOSE:** This course is designed for ongoing and special interest groups. The goal is to get better acquainted and become a support group. Using the analogy of a baseball diamond, the goal of a group is home plate or "bonding." To get to home plate, the group needs to go around three bases: 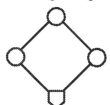 FIRST BASE: History Giving—telling your "story" to one another—your childhood, your journey, your hopes and dreams. SECOND BASE: Affirmation—responding to each other's story with appreciation. THIRD BASE: Need Sharing—going deeper in your story—your present struggles, roadblocks, anxieties, and where you need help from God and the group.

---

**2. AGENDA:** There are three parts to every group meeting:

| **GATHERING** / 10 min. | **BIBLE STUDY** / 30 min. | **CARING** / 20 min. |
|:---:|:---:|:---:|
| Purpose: To break the ice and become better acquainted | Purpose: To share your spiritual journey | Purpose: To share prayer requests and pray |
|  |  |  |

---

**3. FEARLESS FOURSOME:** If you have more than seven in your group at any time, call the option play when the time comes for Bible Study, and subdivide into groups of four for greater participation. (In four's, everyone will share and you can finish the Bible Study in 30 minutes.) Then regather the group for the Caring Time.

| **GATHERING** | **BIBLE STUDY** | **CARING** |
|:---:|:---:|:---:|
| All Together | Groups of 4 | Back Together |
|  |  |  |

---

**4. EMPTY CHAIR:** Pull up an empty chair during the **Caring Time** at the close and ask God to fill this chair each week. Remember, by breaking into groups of four for the Bible Study time, you can grow numerically without feeling "too big" as a group.

The Group Leader needs an Apprentice in training at all times so that the Apprentice can start a new "cell" when the group size is 12 or more.

# SESSION 1
# Orientation

**PURPOSE:** To get acquainted, to share your expectations, and to decide on the ground rules for your group.

**AGENDA:**  Gathering  📖 Bible Study  ♡ Caring Time

**OPEN**

## 📖 GATHERING/10 Minutes/All Together

*Leader: The purpose of the Gathering time is to break the ice. Read the instructions for Step One and go first. Then read the Introduction (Step Two) and the instructions for the Bible Study.*

**Step One: I AM SOMEBODY WHO...** Look over this list and mark five things which describe you. When everyone is finished, put your booklet in a stack in the middle of the group. After the booklets are piled up, pass them out randomly to everyone. Go around the group and take turns reading the five things marked in each booklet, and see if the group can guess who the booklet belongs to. (You'll find this and many other ice-breakers in Serendipity's *Ice-Breakers and Heart-Warmers*.)

I am somebody who:
- ❐ blushes at a compliment.
- ❐ would go on a blind date.
- ❐ likes to travel alone.
- ❐ sings in the shower.
- ❐ saves for a rainy day.
- ❐ slurps my soup.
- ❐ listens to music full blast.
- ❐ likes to dance.
- ❐ cries at movies.
- ❐ stops to smell the flowers.
- ❐ goes to bed early.
- ❐ would enjoy skydiving.
- ❐ cheats at Monopoly.
- ❐ hates flying.
- ❐ falls in love quickly.
- ❐ likes thunderstorms.
- ❐ is afraid of the dark.
- ❐ sleeps until the last second.
- ❐ asks a stranger for directions.
- ❐ enjoys a professional massage.
- ❐ reads the financial page.
- ❐ will tell someone their fly is open.
- ❐ lies about my age.
- ❐ yells at the umpire.
- ❐ fixes my own car.
- ❐ closes my eyes at horror movies.
- ❐ daydreams a lot.
- ❐ avoids discussions about sex.
- ❐ makes a "to do" list each day.
- ❐ loves crossword puzzles.
- ❐ watches soap operas.
- ❐ has never had an operation.
- ❐ always sends greeting cards.
- ❐ will try new dishes at a restaurant.

**Shalom defined**

**Step Two: WELCOME.** Welcome to this course on wholeness. In this course, we have tried to integrate the "holistic health" concepts with the biblical concept of "wholeness." Our justification for this is the word *shalom*, translated "peace" in the New Testament and offered as a free gift to the disciples in John 14:27: "Peace is what I leave with you. It is my own peace that I give you." *Shalom* is the Hebrew word that means inner peace, tranquility, harmony, health, and well-being. *Shalom* is the code-breaking secret that links the holistic health movement with the divine purpose and plan of God.

We have taken the liberty to spell the word "holistic" with a "w," signifying the larger meaning of "wholeness" that can only come through the gift of *shalom*. We have been created for *shalom*. True wholeness is elusive—yet it is attainable. In the following studies, we will consider the wholeness offered by Jesus. He offers us wholeness for our bodies, our minds, and our spirits. In a world which is frail, fractured, and frazzled, this truly is good news!

Each session examines a different dimension of a whole person:
- spiritual: at-one-ment with God
- physical: the temple of God
- vocational: finding the music at work
- emotional: harmony
- relational: members one of another
- volitional: taking charge of your world

The purpose of this course is to put all the parts of our being into "oneness," and in harmony with the Great Physician. Unfortunately, a few of the books about "holistic medicine" have reduced the spiritual dimension into a nebulous meditation technique ("centering"). This may be good therapy, but it cannot replace the healing process that comes from knowing the source of all life and health—God Almighty.

**Three parts to a session**

Every session has three parts: (1) **Gathering**—to break the ice and introduce the topic, (2) **Bible Study**—to share your own story through a passage of Scripture, and (3) **Caring**—to decide what action you need to take in this area of your life, and to support one another in this action.

# 📖 BIBLE STUDY/30 Minutes/Groups of 4

*Leader: If you have more than seven in this session, we recommend groups of four—four to sit around the dining table, four around the kitchen table, and four around a folding table. Ask one person in each foursome to be the Convener and complete the Bible Study in the time allotted. Then regather for the Caring Time, allowing 20 minutes.*

**STUDY**

In each foursome, ask someone to be the Convener. Read the following Scripture and poem based on this passage. Go around on the first question. Then go around with the next question, working through the questionnaire. After 30 minutes, the Leader will call time and ask you to regather for the Caring Time.

*¹ **Praise the LORD, O my soul;**
   **all my inmost being, praise his holy name.**
² **Praise the LORD, O my soul,**
   **and forget not all his benefits—**
³ **who forgives all your sins**
   **and heals all your diseases,**
⁴ **who redeems your life from the pit**
   **and crowns you with love and con. assion,**
⁵ **who satisfies your desires with good things**
   **so that your youth is renewed like the eagle's.**
      **Psalm 103:1–5, NIV***

Lord, I saw myself the other day
   in an overweight, out-of-tune
   gas-guzzling wreck of a car
   chugging along on one
cylinder in the fast lane:
      sputtering... fuming...
      polluting the world with
poison from its own
      internal combustion system.
Lord, before it's too late,
   I'd like a complete overhaul,
   a major tune-up
on this stress machine of mine.
Give me an estimate of the cost!

1. With which of the two poems above do you identify?
   ❒ the Scripture      ❒ "The Gas Guzzler"   ❒ a little of both

2. Of the benefits the psalmist says we receive from the Lord, which do you need the most?
   ❒ spiritual ("forgives all your sins")
   ❒ physical ("heals all your diseases")
   ❒ vocational ("redeems your life from the pit")
   ❒ emotional ("crowns you with... compassion")
   ❒ relational ("crowns you with love")
   ❒ volitional ("satisfies your desires with good things"—by guiding your choices)

3.  If you could compare your life right now to an eagle, where would you be?
    - ❐ soaring high—carried along by the wind
    - ❐ feeling a little turbulence—but I'm making it
    - ❐ tuckered out—it's been a long flight
    - ❐ wounded—buckshot wounds

4.  What aspect of your youth would you like to see renewed?
    - ❐ an attitude of relative trust and innocence in relationships
    - ❐ physical flexibility and stamina
    - ❐ a childlike belief in God
    - ❐ relative freedom from responsibility
    - ❐ a sense of wonder about life

5.  The Psalmist was enthusiastic in his praise. Which of the following would you praise with similar enthusiasm?
    - ❐ my favorite sports figure
    - ❐ my boss
    - ❐ my spouse
    - ❐ my children
    - ❐ my favorite singer or group
    - ❐ my parents
    - ❐ a popular speaker
    - ❐ a mentor/friend
    - ❐ a self-help expert
    - ❐ other: _____

6.  Indicate whether you agree or disagree with each statement below:

| | Agree | Disagree |
|---|---|---|
| Don't go to the doctor if you want to get well. | ❐ | ❐ |
| The church has a very narrow view of what it means to be a whole person. | ❐ | ❐ |
| Living in harmony with myself and living in harmony with God are one and the same. | ❐ | ❐ |
| The modern "holistic health" movement leaves out God, the atonement of Jesus Christ, and the work of the Holy Spirit in achieving maximum well-being. | ❐ | ❐ |
| Jesus Christ came to make me whole. | ❐ | ❐ |
| Headaches, indigestion, insomnia, stomach aches, and ulcers are symptoms of spiritual, physical, or emotional disharmony. | ❐ | ❐ |

**7.** Assume for a moment that the line below represents the two extremes of health. At one extreme is Degenerative Disease/Imminent Death. At the other extreme is Optimum Health/Well-Being. The midpoint on the line would be "normative"; that is, you are not "sick." You are able to function like a normal human being. Put an "✗" on the lines below to indicate where you see yourself in each area.

Degenerative Disease/                                    Optimum Health/
Imminent Death                                           Well-Being

---

ILLNESS                    NORMATIVE                    WHOLENESS

**SPIRITUALLY:** Experiencing the fullness of God's grace and forgiveness.

---

ILLNESS                    NORMATIVE                    WHOLENESS

**PHYSICALLY:** Keeping fit and feeling good.

---

ILLNESS                    NORMATIVE                    WHOLENESS

**EMOTIONALLY:** Coping with tension/stress.

---

ILLNESS                    NORMATIVE                    WHOLENESS

**RELATIONALLY:** Forgiving as Christ forgave me.

---

ILLNESS                    NORMATIVE                    WHOLENESS

**VOCATIONALLY:** Finding fulfillment in my work.

---

ILLNESS                    NORMATIVE                    WHOLENESS

**VOLITIONALLY:** Taking responsibility for my life.

---

ILLNESS                    NORMATIVE                    WHOLENESS

## ♡ CARING TIME/20 Minutes/All Together

*Leader: In this first session, take some time to discuss your expectations and to decide on the ground rules for your group. Then spend the remaining time in caring support for each other through sharing and prayer.*

1. What motivated you to come to this group?
   - ❐ curiosity
   - ❐ A friend asked me.
   - ❐ I had nothing better to do.
   - ❐ a nagging suspicion that I'd better get my life together

2. As you begin this group, what are some goals or expectations you have for this course? Choose two or three of the following expectations and add one of your own:
   - ❐ to discover ways to take care of myself
   - ❐ to take an objective inventory of my life in all its dimensions
   - ❐ to get to know some people who are willing to be open and honest about their struggles with whol-i-ness
   - ❐ to relax and have fun—and forget wholeness for awhile
   - ❐ to see what the Bible has to say about whol-i-ness, the strategies for becoming whole, and achieving *shalom*
   - ❐ to deal with some issues in my life that keep me from whol-i-ness
   - ❐ to see if God is saying anything to me about my life and his will for me
   - ❐ to see if I want to stay in the job I am in right now, or look for something else
   - ❐ to deal with some of the relationships in my life
   - ❐ other: _____

**GROUND RULES**

3. If you are going to commit the next six weeks or sessions to this group, what are some things you want understood by the group before you commit? Check two or three, and add any of your own:

   - ❐ **Attendance**: To take the group seriously, and to give the meetings priority.

   - ❐ **Confidentiality**: Anything that is said in the meetings will not be repeated outside the group.

   - ❐ **Accountability**: The group has the right to hold any member accountable for goals that member sets for himself/herself.

   - ❐ **Responsibility**: Every group member accepts responsibility for the care and encouragement of the other group members.

   - ❐ **Openness**: The group is open to any person who is willing to accept the ground rules.

   - ❐ **Duration**: The group will commit to six more sessions. After this, the group will evaluate and recommit to another period if they wish to do so.

**SHARING** | Take a few minutes to share prayer requests with other group members. Go around and answer this question first:

*"How can we help you in prayer this week?"*

**PRAYER** | Take a moment to pray together. If you have not prayed out loud before, finish the sentence:

*"Hello, God, this is ... (first name). I want to thank you for ..."*

**ACTION** | 1. Decide where you are going to meet.

2. Ask someone to bring refreshments next week.

3. Encourage the group to invite a friend to the group next week—to fill the "empty chair" (see page 5).

# SESSION 2
# Spiritual Dimension

**PURPOSE:** To discover the depth of the spiritual dimension of life.

**AGENDA:** 🍵 Gathering 📖 Bible Study ♡ Caring Time

OPEN ## 🍵 GATHERING/10 Minutes/All Together

*Leader: Read the instructions for Step One and set the pace by going first. Then read Step Two and move on to the Bible Study.*

**Step One: HOW'S THE WEATHER?** Consider all the different areas of your life. Choose three areas and assign a month of the year to each one. Tell the group what season it is in each area of your life. Feel free to explain why you chose what you did.

☐ romance ☐ career ☐ relational
☐ financial ☐ spiritual ☐ family life
☐ emotional ☐ intellectual ☐ overall

**January:** Cold and snowy, but a new year is on the way.
**February:** The bleakest time of the year; I'm getting tired of the color gray.
**March:** Cold and blustery, but there is a sniff of spring in the air.
**April:** Tumultuous and stormy, but life is breaking out everywhere.
**May:** Spring has spring! The flowers are blooming, and the skies are full of sunlight and cool breezes.
**June:** It's pleasantly warm, things are growing, and people are beginning to take vacations.
**July:** Boy, it's hot—everything is smoldering and oppressive.
**August:** The heat has settled in; we sure could use some rain.
**September:** The first cool breezes of fall can be felt, but it sure is warm; there is change in the air.
**October:** Autumn has arrived; life is beginning to hibernate, but the colors are still beautiful.
**November:** The leaves have fallen and it's getting cold.
**December:** Even though it's cold and desolate-looking outside, the holidays keep things festive.

**Step Two: SPIRITUAL DIMENSION.** We live in a time considered to be a scientific and technological age. However, those terms do not do justice to all that people focus on today. For many of us (perhaps the majority), we have discovered that science and technology can't give us all we are searching for in life. These disciplines can give us certain tools for living, but no direction for living. They can describe what is right in front of us, but come up empty in attempts to search the depths of who we really are, and how we are connected with the rest of life.

We are searching for more than science and technology can give us. Because we are searching in a society which has for so long denied the reality of anything beyond the physical, our hunger is especially intense. The only problem is, we are uncertain where to find it! Our increased hunger has driven us to seek answers in astrology, connection with the earth (in Native American religion), and an understanding of life beyond the physical (through New Age mysticism). While these avenues satisfy some, they leave many others confused and spiritually frustrated. Many are beginning to believe that it is time to rediscover biblical Christianity and the importance of the spiritual dimension of our life. That is what this session will help us to do.

**LEADER: Choose the Option One Bible Study (below) or the Option Two Study (page 17).**

In this course, we will challenge you to think in terms of a new paradigm (a model, standard, or ideal) and what it means to be a whole person— HOLY, WHOLLY, HOLEY. In the Bible Study, you will be given two options in each session: (1) Option One—for beginner groups and (2) Option Two—for deeper groups. In the Option One Study (from John's Gospel), we meet a very religious person who came to Jesus at night to ask an honest question about spirituality. In the Option Two Study (from First Corinthians), Paul instructs the Corinthians on the secret wisdom of God—a wisdom not of this age.

**OPTION 1**

 # BIBLE STUDY/30 Minutes/Groups of 4

*Leader: Help the group make a decision for Option One or Option Two. If there are seven or more in your group, quickly subdivide into four's and rearrange your chairs, so that everyone can participate in the Bible Study and discussion. Ask one person in each foursome to be the Convener and complete the Bible Study in the time allotted. Then regather for the Caring Time, allowing 20 minutes.*

# Gospel Study/Night Caller
## John 3:1–21

Read John 3:1–21 and discuss your responses to the following questions with your group. This Bible story is about the difference between being religious and being spiritual.

**3** Now there was a man of the Pharisees named Nicodemus, a member of the Jewish ruling council. [2] He came to Jesus at night and said, "Rabbi, we know you are a teacher who has come from God. For no one could perform the miraculous signs you are doing if God were not with him."

[3] In reply Jesus declared, "I tell you the truth, no one can see the kingdom of God unless he is born again."

[4] "How can a man be born when he is old?" Nicodemus asked. "Surely he cannot enter a second time into his mother's womb to be born!"

[5] Jesus answered, "I tell you the truth, no one can enter the kingdom of God unless he is born of water and the Spirit. [6] Flesh gives birth to flesh, but the Spirit gives birth to spirit. [7] You should not be surprised at my saying, 'You must be born again.' [8] The wind blows wherever it pleases. You hear its sound, but you cannot tell where it comes from or where it is going. So it is with everyone born of the Spirit."

[9] "How can this be?" Nicodemus asked.

[10] "You are Israel's teacher," said Jesus, "and do you not understand these things? [11] I tell you the truth, we speak of what we know, and we testify to what we have seen, but still you people do not accept our testimony. [12] I have spoken to you of earthly things and you do not believe; how then will you believe if I speak of heavenly things? [13] No one has ever gone into heaven except the one who came from heaven—the Son of Man. [14] Just as Moses lifted up the snake in the desert, so the Son of Man must be lifted up, [15] that everyone who believes in him may have eternal life.

[16] "For God so loved the world that he gave his one and only Son, that whoever believes in him shall not perish but have eternal life. [17] For God did not send his Son into the world to condemn the world, but to save the world through him. [18] Whoever believes in him is not condemned, but whoever does not believe stands condemned already because he has not believed in the name of God's one and only Son. [19] This is the verdict: Light has come into the world, but men loved darkness instead of light because their deeds were evil. [20] Everyone who does evil hates the light, and will not come into the light for fear that his deeds will be exposed. [21] But whoever lives by the truth comes into the light, so that it may be seen plainly that what he has done has been done through God."

*John 3:1–21, NIV*

1. As you have observed him in this passage, where do you think Nicodemus would fall on the following lines? (Mark an "N" on each line.)

   a seeker _____ a giver of answers

   open-minded _____ closed-minded

   showing his true self _____ hiding his true self

   spiritually-minded _____ materially-minded

2. Now mark an "M" where you see yourself on the same lines.

3. Why do you think Nicodemus began by affirming that Jesus was "from God"?
   ☐ He believed in affirming people.
   ☐ Nicodemus wanted to show he wasn't like the other Pharisees who rejected Jesus.
   ☐ He wanted to win Jesus' favor, so that Jesus would empathize with his searching.
   ☐ He was setting Jesus up to try to make him look foolish.
   ☐ He was just saying what he believed.

4. What did Jesus mean when he said that one must be "born again" to see the kingdom of God?
   ☐ You have to be an evangelical Christian.
   ☐ You have to be able to point to a specific "conversion experience."
   ☐ Like Bob Dylan said, "He who isn't busy being born, is busy dying."
   ☐ Our spirits are destroyed by sin and hate, and they need God's help to be reborn.
   ☐ other: _____

5. Which of the following phrases describe where you are on your spiritual journey?
   ☐ I'm not on one!
   ☐ I'm just starting out and looking for the map!
   ☐ I've thrown all the maps away, I'm totally lost, and the trip is getting on my nerves!
   ☐ I'm well down the path, but I'm confused by the forks in the road.
   ☐ I'm taking the high road and enjoying the view.
   ☐ I've nearly arrived.

*"We live in a 'fast food' culture. We are overfed and undernourished on almost every level of existence: physical, emotional, intellectual and spiritual."*
—Albert M. Wells Jr.

**6.** What do you think is the most important point in this passage for those who are seeking something more spiritually?
- ❏ Spiritual rebirth is possible. (vv. 3–7)
- ❏ Heaven is waiting for those who believe in Jesus Christ. (vv. 14–16)
- ❏ God does not desire to condemn us, but to save us. (vv. 17–18)
- ❏ If we are open to be enlightened, light will come. (vv. 19–21)

**7.** Which of the following describes your openness to the light God might shed on your journey?
- ❏ There's still a lot of me that I want to hide in darkness.
- ❏ I want to leave the darkness, but the light hurts my eyes.
- ❏ It's so dark I can't find a light.
- ❏ I see some light, but it seems so faint.
- ❏ The more I follow the light, the brighter it becomes.
- ❏ God has brought all the light that I need to my world.

**8.** Which of the following statements describes what you want out of life? Which one describes what you are actually getting out of life? Where do you feel "cheated"? Why?

LEADER: When you have completed the ble Study, move on to the Caring Time (page 20).

| | what I want | what I'm getting | where I feel cheated |
|---|---|---|---|
| I want my life to be as safe and secure as possible. | ❏ | ❏ | ❏ |
| I want to be as emotionally satisfied as possible. | ❏ | ❏ | ❏ |
| I want to be as intellectually aware as possible. | ❏ | ❏ | ❏ |
| I want to be as spiritually mature as possible. | ❏ | ❏ | ❏ |
| I want to "have it all"— physically, spiritually, vocationally, emotionally, and relationally. | ❏ | ❏ | ❏ |

OPTION 2

# Epistle Study/More Than New Age
## 1 Corinthians 2:6–16

STUDY

Read 1 Corinthians 2:6–16 and share your responses to the questions with your group. Paul qualifies what he just said about his rejection of human wisdom (vv. 4–5). There is, in fact, a legitimate "message of wisdom," but it comes from God and is discerned only by those who have the Spirit.

*⁶ We do, however, speak a message of wisdom among the mature, but not the wisdom of this age or of the rulers of this age, who are coming to nothing. ⁷ No, we speak of God's secret wisdom, a wisdom that has been hidden and that God destined for our glory before time began. ⁸ None of the rulers of this age understood it, for if they had, they would not have crucified the Lord of glory. ⁹ However, as it is written:*

> *"No eye has seen,*
> *no ear has heard,*
> *no mind has conceived*
> *what God has prepared for those who love him"—*

*¹⁰ but God has revealed it to us by his Spirit.*

*The Spirit searches all things, even the deep things of God. ¹¹ For who among men knows the thoughts of a man except the man's spirit within him? In the same way no one knows the thoughts of God except the Spirit of God. ¹² We have not received the spirit of the world but the Spirit who is from God, that we may understand what God has freely given us. ¹³ This is what we speak, not in words taught us by human wisdom but in words taught by the Spirit, expressing spiritual truths in spiritual words. ¹⁴ The man without the Spirit does not accept the things that come from the Spirit of God, for they are foolishness to him, and he cannot understand them, because they are spiritually discerned. ¹⁵ The spiritual man makes judgments about all things, but he himself is not subject to any man's judgment:*

> *¹⁶ "For who has known the mind of the Lord*
> *that he may instruct him?"*

*But we have the mind of Christ.*

*1 Corinthians 2:6–16, NIV*


1. How would you summarize the message of this passage?
   - ❏ Spiritual wisdom differs from what the secular world calls wisdom.
   - ❏ To understand spiritual matters, God's Spirit must teach you.
   - ❏ Spiritual matters seem like foolishness to those who are only focused on the material world.
   - ❏ other: _____

2. For a person who is seeking spiritual truth, how important is wisdom from secular sources?
   - ❏ It's not important at all.
   - ❏ It should be secondary to God's direction.
   - ❏ It's very important—God gave us our minds to use.

3. Who in your life has epitomized wisdom for you? What did he or she teach you that has remained with you?

4. Which of the following sources of wisdom have given you guidance and help in your spiritual journey? (Mark as many as apply.)
   ❐ the Bible
   ❐ psychology or self-help literature
   ❐ classics like Shakespeare
   ❐ Christian devotional literature
   ❐ secular novels like *The Brothers Karamozov*
   ❐ children's books, like *The Velveteen Rabbit*
   ❐ Christian novels, like *This Present Darkness*
   ❐ the classic philosophers, like Plato
   ❐ other: _____

5. What practices or spiritual disciplines have helped you cultivate the spiritual dimension of your life?
   ❐ yoga
   ❐ spiritual meditation
   ❐ daily Scripture reading
   ❐ praying the Scripture
   ❐ being in a small group
   ❐ going to Mass or some service of worship

6. How would you describe the "wisdom of this age"? (Choose the two which are most appropriate.)
   ❐ materially-focused    ❐ not biblically based
   ❐ shortsighted          ❐ focused on selfish advantage
   ❐ changing constantly   ❐ excludes God
   ❐ unloving              ❐ not rooted in Christian tradition
   ❐ morally undemanding   ❐ other: _____

7. What helps you to discern between "the wisdom of this age" and God's wisdom for the mature?
   ❐ to pray for the Spirit's guidance
   ❐ to look to the example of Jesus so as to have "the mind of Christ"
   ❐ to read more of the Bible
   ❐ to discuss the matter with other believers
   ❐ other: _____

*"The relationship of a man's soul to God is best evidenced by those things that occupy his thoughts."*
—Kenneth L. Dodge

**LEADER: When you have completed the Bible Study, move on to the Caring Time (below).**

**8.** Although our Scripture says, "no mind has conceived what God has prepared for those who love him," what would you like to see God prepare for you in the future?
- ☐ a life with less personal conflict
- ☐ a life with more intimacy between me and others
- ☐ eternal life with my family and loved ones included
- ☐ a life where love and justice is the rule
- ☐ a life where there is nothing to fear
- ☐ a life where I feel fully connected with all of creation

#  CARING TIME/20 Minutes/All Together

*Leader: The purpose of the Caring Time in this session is to spend time in caring support for each other through Sharing, Prayer, and Action.*

**SHARING**

In *The Wizard of Oz*, the four characters (the Lion, the Tin Man, the Scarecrow, and Dorothy) were each given something new—something to help them. If God could renew something in your life today, what would you ask for? Go around and finish this sentence:

*"I would ask God for ..."*

**PRAYER**

Close with a short time of prayer, remembering the requests that have been shared. If you would like to pray in silence, say the word "Amen" when you have finished your prayer, so that the next person will know when to start.

**ACTION**

Ask each member of the group to write down on an index card their first name and a prayer request concerning their spiritual dimension of wholeness. Randomly distribute the cards and ask each person to pray for the group member on the card throughout the next week.

# SESSION 3
# Physical Dimension

**PURPOSE:** To discover our responsibility for the "preventive maintenance" of our physical bodies.

**AGENDA:**  Gathering  Bible Study  Caring Time

**OPEN**

#  GATHERING/10 Minutes/All Together

*Leader: Read the instructions for Step One and set the pace by going first. Then read the Introduction in Step Two and move on to the Bible Study.*

**Step One: PHYSICAL CHECKUP.** Before you get into the Bible Study, take a moment and check to see how healthy your lifestyle is right now. Circle where you are in each category. Share your responses with the group.

| | EXCELLENT | GOOD | FAIR | POOR | DANGEROUS |
|---|---|---|---|---|---|
| **SMOKING** | Never smoked, or have stopped smoking | Less than 10 cigarettes per day, not inhaled | Less than 10 cigarettes per day, inhaled | 10–19 cigarettes per day | 20 or more cigarettes per day |
| **ALCOHOL** | Less than 7 drinks per week; judgment never impaired | 7–14 drinks per week; judgment rarely impaired | 15–21 drinks per week; judgment occasionally impaired | 22–35 drinks per week; judgment sometimes impaired | More than 35 drinks per week; judgment frequently impaired |
| **TRIMNESS** | Lean | Slightly overweight | Moderately overweight | Considerably overweight | Grossly overweight |
| **PHYSICAL ACTIVITY** | Consistently active (equivalent to 2–5 miles daily) | Moderately active (equivalent to 1.5–2 miles daily) | Some exercise (equivalent to 1–1.5 miles daily) | Seldom exercise (equivalent to 0.5–1 mile daily) | Sedentary (less than 0.5 mile daily) |
| **NON-PRESCRIPTION DRUGS** | Only on doctor's orders; never mixed with alcohol | Used occasionally for short period only; alcohol not used at same time | More frequent use for long periods; no alcohol used at same time | Used frequently; mixed with alcohol | Continually used; mixed with alcohol |
| **TRANQUILITY** | Generally relaxed; able to relieve stress by exercise or recreation | Generally relaxed; sometimes able to relieve stress | Moderate degree of stress | Easily stressed; not able to relieve stress or sleep it off | Continually stressed |
| **BLOOD CHOLESTEROL, GLUCOSE, AND BLOOD PRESSURE** | Measured every 2 years, or as prescribed by doctor—conscientious diet | Measured 2–5 years; watch diet but not consistent | Every 5 years; have cut out some foods that can be harmful | Aware, but unable to control eating habits | Never; don't care about what is eaten |

**Step Two: PHYSICAL DIMENSION.** We do not usually appreciate our physical health until we lose it. It may only be the aches, nausea, and general malaise of the flu which causes us to stop and think about how wonderful physical health is. Or it may be a chronic, debilitating condition which permanently alters our lives, and causes us to forget what physical wholeness ever felt like. Whatever our current condition, it's important for us to be attentive to our physical health and well-being.

We also tend to forget that there is a connection between our physical and our spiritual health. Apart from anything else, when we are ill, we cannot be involved in ministry in the same way as when we are healthy. Furthermore, our emotions are often out of kilter then, and our minds don't work as well as they normally do. Have you ever tried to pray when you have a fever? God has given us wonderful bodies with amazing capabilities. Part of our spiritual responsibility is to keep them in good condition.

**LEADER: Choose the Option One Bible Study (below) or the Option Two Study (page 26).**

Jesus understood the importance of physical health. Not only did he heal many who were sick and debilitated, but he also understood the importance of taking care of a healthy body. In the following Option One Study (from John's Gospel), Jesus encountered a man who was crippled for 38 years. The healing Jesus brings to this man included more than restoring his ability to walk. In the Option Two Study, the Psalmist David appeals to God for relief from a severe and painful illness.

**OPTION 1**

 # BIBLE STUDY/30 Minutes/Groups of 4

*Leader: Help the group decide to choose Option One or Option Two for their Bible Study. If there are seven or more in the group, encourage them to move into groups of four. Ask one person in each group to be the Convener. The Convener guides the sharing and makes sure that each group member has an opportunity to answer every question.*

## Gospel Study/Tough Question
## John 5:1–9

**STUDY**

Jesus practiced a little wholistic medicine in this passage. We don't know the whole story here, but it appears that the patient was more than just physically crippled. Read John 5:1–9 and discuss your responses to the following questions with your group.

**5** Some time later, Jesus went up to Jerusalem for a feast of the Jews. ² Now there is in Jerusalem near the Sheep Gate a pool, which in Aramaic is called Bethesda and which is surrounded by five covered colonnades. ³ Here a great number of disabled people used to lie—the blind, the lame, the paralyzed. ⁵ One who was there had been an invalid for thirty-eight years. ⁶ When Jesus saw him lying there and learned that he had been in this condition for a long time, he asked him, "Do you want to get well?"

⁷ "Sir," the invalid replied, "I have no one to help me into the pool when the water is stirred. While I am trying to get in, someone else goes down ahead of me."

⁸ Then Jesus said to him, "Get up! Pick up your mat and walk." ⁹ At once the man was cured; he picked up his mat and walked.

*John 5:1–9, NIV*

1. Assume for a moment that you are a social worker for the Public Health Department in Jerusalem. You have been assigned to investigate a welfare case described in this passage. Read the Scripture carefully for clues to this person's illness. Then fill in this welfare report.

*According to one study, 50 percent of the people occupying hospital beds today, and 90 percent of people who regularly call the doctor, are not medically sick. They may hurt, but the cause of their pain is not physical. These kinds of illnesses are called psycho-somatic—sickness caused by the mind or outside circumstances.*

**CASE:** 4765
**RESIDENCE:** Unknown
**WHEREABOUTS:**
**CONDITION OF PATIENT:**

| PHYSICAL SYMPTOMS | EMOTIONAL SYMPTOMS | SPIRITUAL SYMPTOMS |
|---|---|---|
| ❏ high blood pressure | ❏ irritability | ❏ poor self-esteem |
| ❏ creeping obesity | ❏ anxiety, tension, worry | ❏ worthless |
| ❏ insomnia | ❏ low-grade depression | ❏ self-centered pity |
| ❏ chronic fatigue | ❏ escapism | ❏ lack of initiative |
| ❏ persistent headaches | ❏ avoidance behavior | ❏ alienated from reality |
| ❏ partial paralysis | ❏ fright/flight behavior | ❏ hopeless |
| ❏ gastrointestinal distress, frequent indigestion, and constipation | ❏ irresponsible | ❏ self-righteous |
|  | ❏ extreme dependence | ❏ condemning of self |
|  | ❏ withdrawn | ❏ laziness |
| ❏ frequent colds | ❏ paranoid | ❏ haughtiness |
| ❏ sinuses | ❏ suicidal | ❏ neurotic guilt |
| ❏ skin irritation | ❏ exhibitionism | ❏ lack of joy |
| ❏ drowsiness | ❏ out of touch with reality |  |
| ❏ chills/perspiration | ❏ blames others |  |
| ❏ back pain |  |  |
| ❏ hysterical paralysis |  |  |

---

**TREATMENT:** Study how Jesus dealt with this man. Check two things Jesus did with him.

❏ exposed the man as a con artist
❏ rescued the man and coddled him
❏ permitted him to heal himself
❏ affirmed the worth of this person
❏ comforted this man with a placebo
❏ accepted this person as he was

❏ refused to allow him to play games
❏ healed something inside this person
❏ performed a miracle
❏ stripped the person of his excuses
❏ confronted him with his real problem
❏ allowed the man to take responsibility for
his own health

---

2. If you were a news reporter for *The Jerusalem Journal*, what would you write as a headline in the late edition?
   ❏ "Healer Asks Cripple, 'Do you want to get well?' "
   ❏ "Healer Embarrasses Cripple Before Healing Him"
   ❏ "Cripple at Bethesda Healed After 38 Years"
   ❏ "Strange Rabbi Orders Cripple to Move It!"

3. Which statement best describes how you feel about physical fitness?
   ❏ Staying physically fit is very important to me.
   ❏ I leave physical fitness to the young.
   ❏ Physical fitness is overrated in our society.
   ❏ I worry about it, but only exercise sporadically.
   ❏ When I feel like exercising, I lay down until the feeling goes away.
   ❏ Physical fitness should be balanced with emotional and spiritual fitness.

4. How did the crippled man respond to Jesus?
   ❏ "Are you crazy? Would I be lying here for 38 years if I could walk?"
   ❏ "O poor me; I'm really so helpless."
   ❏ "Others that I have relied on have failed me."
   ❏ "I've been sick for so long I don't think I can accept responsibility for my life."

5. What was Jesus really saying when he said: "Get up, pick up your mat, and walk"?
   ❏ If you really want to get well, you can.
   ❏ Don't blame others for your problems.
   ❏ I'm sick of your whining—move it!
   ❏ Getting well may cost you your excuses—are you willing to risk it?
   ❏ I have removed all of the obstacles—get moving!
   ❏ other: _____

**6.** What connection have you noticed between your physical and spiritual health?

☐ My physical health only lasts if I am spiritually well.

☐ My physical health is sometimes related to my spiritual health.

☐ My physical health is helped by spiritual remedies.

☐ A prayer a day keeps the doctor away.

**7.** Have you ever become physically sick over problems you refused to deal with? What happened?

**8.** If Jesus passed by your "pool" today, what would he say or do?

☐ He would congratulate me on taking care of myself.

☐ He would warn me about my physical fitness.

☐ He would tell me to stop complaining.

☐ He would ask me the same questions.

☐ Other: _____

**LEADER: When you have completed the Bible Study, move on to the Caring Time (page 28).**

**9.** Dr. Lester Breslow, dean of UCLA's School of Public Health, found that seven basic living habits are crucial to health. People with all seven habits are healthier than those with six; those with six are more healthy than those with five, etc. Check to see how you measure up:

☐ moderate, regular exercise  ☐ 7–8 hours of sleep each night

☐ normal weight   ☐ moderate drinking

☐ breakfast every day   ☐ no smoking

☐ regular meals with no snacks between meals

**COMMENT**

We don't know why this man was paralyzed for 38 years. But we do know that Jesus addressed more than just his physical needs. After being ill for this extended period of time, the man must have developed other problems as well. Many of us become cranky and irritable if we have to spend a few days in bed with the flu.

This is also a story of expectations. The man did not know about Jesus or his reputation as a healer. He hoped that Jesus would help him into the pool when the angels came to stir the waters. Instead Jesus healed him, forgave his sins, and brought wholeness to his life. Jesus' desire is to do the same for us as he encourages us to take care of ourselves.

25

# Epistle Study/Body Language
## Psalm 38:1–8

Read Psalm 38:1–8. Psalms were poems that were often used in worship in ancient times. They had different moods—some were full of praise to God; some were appeals to God for strength or healing. This poem is of the latter type. Discuss the questions which follow with your group.

> *¹ O LORD, do not rebuke me in your anger*
> *    or discipline me in your wrath.*
> *² For your arrows have pierced me,*
> *    and your hand has come down upon me.*
> *³ Because of your wrath there is no health in my body;*
> *    my bones have no soundness because of my sin.*
> *⁴ My guilt has overwhelmed me*
> *    like a burden too heavy to bear.*
>
> *⁵ My wounds fester and are loathsome*
> *    because of my sinful folly.*
> *⁶ I am bowed down and brought very low;*
> *    all day long I go about mourning.*
> *⁷ My back is filled with searing pain;*
> *    there is no health in my body.*
> *⁸ I am feeble and utterly crushed;*
> *    I groan in anguish of heart.*
>
> *Psalm 38:1–8, NIV*

1. How would you compare the way your body feels right now to the description of the psalmist in the Scripture?
   - ❑ We are about the same.
   - ❑ He was probably feeling worse.
   - ❑ I am probably feeling worse.

2. Which of the following best describes how you think about your physical health?
   - ❑ I worry about it.
   - ❑ I don't give it a second thought.
   - ❑ I do what I can to stay healthy .
   - ❑ I am probably not as conscientious as I should be.
   - ❑ I take it for granted.
   - ❑ I give it top priority.

**3.** Which of the following do you do to safeguard your physical health?

☐ get regular physical exams  ☐ eat a balanced, low-fat diet
☐ keep my cholesterol down  ☐ exercise regularly
☐ avoid smoking  ☐ drink alcohol in moderation
☐ drink plenty of water  ☐ avoid illegal drugs
☐ get plenty of rest  ☐ other: _____

**4.** Why do you think the psalmist saw a connection between physical health and spiritual health?

☐ Because he was from a primitive, superstitious culture.
☐ Because he saw certain symptoms occurring together and made the connection.
☐ Because God had revealed a connection to him.
☐ other: _____

**5.** Pick three of the "spiritual symptoms" and three of the "physical symptoms" below that you have experienced in the last month, and circle each. Share them with your group. Then share any connection you see where the spiritual symptoms might cause or aggravate the physical symptoms (or vice versa):

| SPIRITUAL SYMPTOMS | PHYSICAL SYMPTOMS |
|---|---|
| estrangement | insomnia |
| meaningless | headache |
| empty | clammy |
| guilty | tense |
| depressed | crippled |
| unclean | torn |
| dry | overwhelmed |
| wounded | lazy |
| alienated | ulcerated |
| disillusioned | exhausted |
| impoverished | paralyzed |
| desolate | suicidal |
| worthless | knotted up |
| helpless | indigestion |
| homeless | hot flashes |
| restless | chills |
| hopeless | distraught |
| down | constipation |

6. Early in life, St. Francis of Assisi referred to his body disrespectfully as "Brother Ass." But as he grew older, he referred to his body as "Brother Friend." Put an "**X**" someplace in between these two extremes to indicate how you view your body:

Brother Ass _____ Brother Friend

**LEADER: When you have completed the Bible Study, move on to the Caring Time (below).**

7. How do you think you would react if your physical health and wholeness were lost? How would this change your life? How would it affect your relationships?

8. Which of the following has caused you to "groan in anguish of heart" recently? How do you think this matter has affected your health?
   ❒ death of friend or a loved one
   ❒ a broken relationship
   ❒ a professional failure
   ❒ a serious world or community problem
   ❒ problems in disciplining the children
   ❒ financial stress
   ❒ other: _____

#  CARING TIME/20 Minutes/All Together

*Leader: Bring all of the foursomes back together for a time of caring. Follow the three steps below.*

**SHARING**

**HONEY FOR MY EARS.** Here is a heart-warmer (closing activity) from Serendipity's *Ice-Breakers and Heart-Warmers*. Has someone ever told you something that made you feel great? What would you like to hear every now and then that would make you feel special?

Choose one of the general statements listed on the next page and tell the group what you would like to hear. Enjoy it as the other group members take turns affirming you.

I really enjoy it when someone says:

- ☐ something that recognizes my abilities.
- ☐ that they've noticed my personal growth.
- ☐ that I've inspired them in some way.
- ☐ something positive about the way I look.
- ☐ that there is something about me they want to emulate.
- ☐ that they care how I feel.
- ☐ something that tells me I'm loved unconditionally.
- ☐ something that tells me I'm forgiven.

**PRAYER**

If your body could put in a prayer request for you today, what would it say? Finish this sentence:

*"Dear God, my body would like to tell you ..."*

Close with a short time of prayer, remembering the requests that have been shared. If you would like to pray in silence, say the word "Amen" when you have finished your prayer, so that the next person will know when to start.

**ACTION**

1. Turn to the person next to you and tell them one thing you want to change this week about your physical self. For example: "Pray that I begin to view my body as God views it," or "Pray that I make necessary changes in my exercise or eating habits," or "Pray that I will make an appointment for a physical."

2. Prayerfully, write down two or three steps to assist you in meeting your above-mentioned request.

# SESSION 4
# Vocational Dimension

**PURPOSE:** To discover the importance of how we view our work and career.

**AGENDA:** 🍵 Gathering  📖 Bible Study  ♡ Caring Time

**OPEN**

## 🍵 GATHERING/10 Minutes/All Together

*Leader: Read the instructions for Step One. Then read Step Two and move on to the Bible Study.*

**Step One: CAREER CHOICES.** Read the list of career choices aloud and quickly choose someone in your group for each job—based upon their unique gifts and talents. Have fun!

_____ Environmental engineer at nudist colony

_____ Supervisor of complaint department for a woman's lingerie store

_____ Animal psychiatrist for depressed dogs

_____ Dance instructor at geriatric nursing home

_____ Librarian for the Graceland Elvis memorabilia

_____ Research scientist studying the spawning habits of Alaskan salmon

_____ Toy assembly person for a local toy store over the holidays

_____ Research scientist testing the support of mattresses

_____ Head technician for Musak tapes (elevator music)

_____ Female TV reporter for male locker room

_____ Surfboarding instructor at a Junior College in Hawaii

_____ Consistency expert for chewing gum manufacturer

_____ Curator for the wax museum of pygmy headhunters

**Step Two: VOCATIONAL DIMENSION.** Go to any gathering of new people and chances are their second question (after "What is your name?") will be, "What do you do for a living?" or "Where do you work?" In our society, a large part of a person's identity is connected to what they do. We all want a job or a career which pays us a lot of money, allows us flexibility, and fulfills us as individuals.

But many Americans find that their jobs do not fulfill these desires. In a survey by James Patterson and Peter Kim (reported in their book, *The Day America Told the Truth*), only one American in ten reported being satisfied with his or her work. Only one in four said they gave their work their best effort. Why is there this disparity between what we want in work and what we experience? Part of it may be our attitude. We need to see our work as more than a paycheck—we need to see it as a true "vocation"; that is, God's calling to use our talents to enrich God's children and God's world. When we can't see our work in this way, it brings stress to our life and that in turn can affect our physical, emotional, and spiritual well-being. This session will help us to see our work as vocation.

**LEADER: Choose the Option One Bible Study (below) or the Option Two Study (page 34).**

In this session, we will study the life of the Apostle Paul. In our Option One Study, we learn of Paul's dramatic conversion and subsequent change in vocation. In the Option Two Study (from Paul's letter to the Galatians), Paul describes how his conversion affected other areas of his life.

**OPTION 1**

# 📖 BIBLE STUDY/30 Minutes/Groups of 4

*Leader: Help the groups decide on an Option One or Option Two Bible Study. If there are more than seven people, divide into groups of four, and ask one person in each group to be the Convener. Finish the Bible Study in 30 minutes, and gather the groups together for the Caring Time.*

## Gospel Study/Career Crisis
## Acts 9:1–19

**STUDY**

Read Acts 9:1–19 and discuss your responses to the following questions with your group. This is the story of the Apostle Paul receiving his call.

**9** *Meanwhile, Saul was still breathing out murderous threats against the Lord's disciples. He went to the high priest ² and asked him for letters to the synagogues in Damascus, so that if he found any there who belonged to the Way, whether men or women, he might take them as prisoners to Jerusalem. ³ As he neared Damascus on his journey, suddenly* *a light from heaven flashed around him. ⁴ He fell to the ground and heard a voice say to him, "Saul, Saul, why do you persecute me?"*

*⁵ "Who are you, Lord?" Saul asked.*

*"I am Jesus, whom you are persecuting," he replied. ⁶ "Now get up and go into the city, and you will be told what you must do."*

*⁷ The men traveling with Saul stood there speechless; they heard the sound but did not see anyone. ⁸ Saul got up from the ground, but when he opened his eyes he could see nothing. So they led him by the hand into Damascus. ⁹ For three days he was blind, and did not eat or drink anything.*

*¹⁰ In Damascus there was a disciple named Ananias. The Lord called to him in a vision, "Ananias!"*

*"Yes, Lord," he answered.*

*¹¹ The Lord told him, "Go to the house of Judas on Straight Street and ask for a man from Tarsus named Saul, for he is praying. ¹² In a vision he has seen a man named Ananias come and place his hands on him to restore his sight."*

*¹³ "Lord," Ananias answered, "I have heard many reports about this man and all the harm he has done to your saints in Jerusalem. ¹⁴ And he has come here with authority from the chief priests to arrest all who call on your name."*

*¹⁵ But the Lord said to Ananias, "Go! This man is my chosen instrument to carry my name before the Gentiles and their kings and before the people of Israel. ¹⁶ I will show him how much he must suffer for my name."*

*¹⁷ Then Ananias went to the house and entered it. Placing his hands on Saul, he said, "Brother Saul, the Lord—Jesus, who appeared to you on the road as you were coming here—has sent me so that you may see again and be filled with the Holy Spirit." ¹⁸ Immediately, something like scales fell from Saul's eyes, and he could see again. He got up and was baptized, ¹⁹ and after taking some food, he regained his strength.*

***Acts 9:1–19, NIV***

**1.** How would the medical profession today explain what happened to Saul (the Apostle Paul) on the road to Damascus?
- ❐ Paul had a physical breakdown.
- ❐ Paul had an emotional breakdown.
- ❐ Paul had a partial stroke that rendered him blind.
- ❐ Paul had a spiritual crisis due to an overly-religious passion.
- ❐ Paul suffered from extreme guilt due to his role in the stoning of Stephen (the first Christian martyr).
- ❐ Paul experienced a temporary blackout because of low blood sugar and irregular eating habits.
- ❐ Paul went through a career crisis that caused him to experience all of the above.

2. How would a career counselor today explain what happened to Paul on the road to Damascus?

3. If you were Paul, which of the following phrases would express the anxieties you might have had about the impact of this experience on your career?
   ☐ "All of that work establishing connections with the high priest—for nothing!"
   ☐ "I wonder how much it pays to set up churches?"
   ☐ "What are my friends and family in Tarsus going to think?"
   ☐ "What if I had that vision because of something I ate?"
   ☐ "How am I going to talk to people I was once trying to arrest?"
   ☐ "What if I fail?"
   ☐ other: _____

4. What is the closest you've come to Paul's experience, when your entire focus in your career changed?
   ☐ I have never experienced anything like this.
   ☐ There was one time when my life focus suddenly changed.
   ☐ There have been a few minor experiences like this when God seemed to intervene.
   ☐ I don't believe God works this way anymore.

5. There was a person that God sent to Paul to help him sort out what he was experiencing. In your career formation, who is the "Ananias" that helped you to sort out what you were experiencing?

6. If you had to compare where you are right now in your career to Paul's experience in this story, where would you be?
   ☐ on the road to Damascus—pursuing my own passion
   ☐ hearing God call my name and wondering what God is trying to tell me
   ☐ experiencing some of the same emotions and physical symptoms that Paul had
   ☐ starting to sort out God's call on my vocational life

7. **SELF-EXAMINATION:** Below is a statement from a medieval monk named Brother Lawrence. He chose to be a monk so that he could pray and sacrifice his life to God. He was sure that it would be a painful life. Instead he found that God met him at every turn, to the extent that the times of prayer were no more "spiritual" than the labor of running the kitchen. He learned that God was as present in work as in prayer; in fact, his work enhanced his prayer.

After reading his statement, put an "**✗**" on the line below to indicate how you view your work or present occupation.

*"The time of business does not differ with me from the time of prayer; and in the noise and clutter of my kitchen, while several persons are at the same time calling for different things, I possess God in as great tranquility as if I were upon my knees at the blessed sacrament."*

I LOOK UPON MY CAREER AS:

**Just a job** _____ **A high calling**
**to endure**                                                                     **from God**

**LEADER: When you have completed the Bible Study, move on to the Caring Time (page 37).**

8. As you look at your vocational future, what "scales" might block your vision of what God wants you to do?
   - ❏ my love of money
   - ❏ my love for the security of the status quo
   - ❏ my inability to see how God could use what I am presently doing
   - ❏ family pressures
   - ❏ my inability to visualize anything different
   - ❏ my lack of openness to God's direction in this area
   - ❏ other: _____

**OPTION 2**

# Epistle Study/Bumpy Road
# Galatians 1:11–2:2

**STUDY**

The Option One Study examined the transformation in the vocational part of Paul's life. This is often described as his "conversion." But it was more than a spiritual conversion. It was a radically new calling in his vocational life, accompanied by physical, emotional, and psychological transformation.

In this Option, you will look back at this transformation in Paul's life in his letter to the Galatians. Here he defends his calling to those who tried to discredit his authority. Read Galatians 1:11–2:2 and use the questions below to explore some vocational issues in Paul's life and your life.

*¹¹ I want you to know, brothers, that the gospel I preached is not something that man made up. ¹² I did not receive it from any man, nor was I taught it; rather, I received it by revelation from Jesus Christ.*

*¹³ For you have heard of my previous way of life in Judaism, how intensely I persecuted the church of God and tried to destroy it. ¹⁴ I was advancing in Judaism beyond many Jews of my own age and was extremely zealous for the traditions of my fathers. ¹⁵ But when God, who set me apart from birth and called me by his grace, was pleased ¹⁶ to reveal his Son in me so that I might preach him among the Gentiles, I did not consult any man, ¹⁷ nor did I go up to Jerusalem to see those who were apostles before I was, but I went immediately into Arabia and later returned to Damascus.*

*¹⁸ Then after three years, I went up to Jerusalem to get acquainted with Peter and stayed with him fifteen days. ¹⁹ I saw none of the other apostles— only James, the Lord's brother. ²⁰ I assure you before God that what I am writing you is no lie. ²¹ Later I went to Syria and Cilicia. ²² I was personally unknown to the churches of Judea that are in Christ. ²³ They only heard the report: "The man who formerly persecuted us is now preaching the faith he once tried to destroy." ²⁴ And they praised God because of me.*

*2 Fourteen years later I went up again to Jerusalem, this time with Barnabas. I took Titus along also. ² I went in response to a revelation and set before them the gospel that I preach among the Gentiles. But I did this privately to those who seemed to be leaders, for fear that I was running or had run my race in vain.*

*Galatians 1:11–2:2, NIV*

1. How long have you known what God called you to do?
   ❑ I've known all along.
   ❑ I knew when I was in high school.
   ❑ I've known for many years.
   ❑ I'm still not sure.

2. From Paul's account, how long do you think it took him to really know what God wanted to do in and through his life?
   ❑ He knew immediately what he was called to do.
   ❑ It probably took him a few days.
   ❑ Maybe he understood after his time in Arabia, in the desert for three years.
   ❑ It probably took all of 14 years and then some.
   ❑ Other: _____

3. Paul said he was "advancing in Judaism beyond many Jews my own age." In what areas do you feel you have advanced beyond other people you know?
   - ❏ professionally
   - ❏ in sports
   - ❏ academically
   - ❏ in cooking
   - ❏ in music
   - ❏ in my ability to organize myself and my home
   - ❏ as a listener
   - ❏ as a spouse
   - ❏ other: _____
   - ❏ financially
   - ❏ in biblical knowledge
   - ❏ in a hobby: _____
   - ❏ in areas of the country where I have traveled
   - ❏ in mechanical ability
   - ❏ as a parent
   - ❏ as a leader
   - ❏ as a communicator

4. On the scale below, how sure does Paul seem to be that God was directing him vocationally?

   | 1 | 2 | 3 | 4 | 5 | 6 | 7 | 8 | 9 | 10 |
   |---|---|---|---|---|---|---|---|---|----|
   | Not at all | | | | Somewhat sure | | | | | Very sure |

5. Using the same scale, how sure are you that God is directing you vocationally?

   | 1 | 2 | 3 | 4 | 5 | 6 | 7 | 8 | 9 | 10 |
   |---|---|---|---|---|---|---|---|---|----|
   | Not at all | | | | Somewhat sure | | | | | Very sure |

6. In verse 15, Paul states that God "set me apart from birth... that I might preach [the gospel]." How would you apply that statement to your life?
   - ❏ It doesn't apply to me, only to Paul.
   - ❏ I think that Paul is taking this transformation thing a bit too far.
   - ❏ Paul didn't have any choice in careers.
   - ❏ I chose my career, not God.
   - ❏ I can see how God prepared me for my career.
   - ❏ other: _____

7. What do you look for in choosing a job? Choose and rank your top three choices:
   - ___ financial security
   - ___ personal fulfillment
   - ___ sharing my gifts
   - ___ environment/location
   - ___ prestige/power
   - ___ opportunity/challenge
   - ___ family life
   - ___ retirement benefits
   - ___ contributions I can make
   - ___ independence

LEADER: When you have completed the Bible Study, move on to the Caring Time (below).

8. Paul provides his work history to show how his conversion experience changed him in dramatic ways. If you had to explain the reality of the gospel by giving one example of how faith in Christ has changed you, what would you share?

9. If you developed a sense of vocation as strong as Paul's, what would you do differently?
   - ❑ work with more care and pride
   - ❑ enjoy my work more
   - ❑ change jobs
   - ❑ think more of the customer (or those who receive my services)
   - ❑ give God the glory, instead of taking it myself
   - ❑ I'd be less discouraged.
   - ❑ Nothing—I have that sense of vocation right now.

#  CARING TIME/20 Minutes/All Together

*Leader: Bring all of the foursomes back together for a time of caring. Follow the three steps below. Be sensitive when others share about their careers and hopes.*

**SHARING**

Go around and let everyone finish one of the sentences below:

*"If I knew that I could not fail, I would like to try ..."*
*"For my present job to be a calling from God, I need to ..."*
*"To do the job Jesus has called me to, I need to ..."*

**PRAYER**

Close with a short time of prayer, remembering the dreams that have been shared. If you would like to pray in silence, say the word "Amen" when you have finished your prayer, so that the next person will know when to start.

**ACTION**

Turn to the person next to you and tell them one thing you want to change this week in order to bring a sense of wholeness to your vocation. For example: "I will be especially kind to my spouse or a difficult co-worker," or "I won't work overtime this week, and I'll take all of my lunch breaks." Throughout the coming week, be in prayer for each other.

# SESSION 5
# Emotional Dimension

**PURPOSE:** To learn to express, understand, and use our emotions in a healthy manner.

**AGENDA:**  Gathering  Bible Study  Caring Time

**OPEN**

##  GATHERING/10 Minutes/All Together

*Leader: Read the Instructions for Step One and go first. Then read the Introduction and explain the Bible Study choices.*

**Step One: MY CHILDHOOD TABLE.** Take a few moments to reminisce about one year in your life—age 7. Answer questions 1–8. Then choose two of the remaining questions (9–16), and share your responses with the group.

At age 7...

1. Where did you live?
2. What was your house like?
3. What was your bedroom like?
4. What was your favorite hiding place?
5. What was your favorite TV/radio program?
6. Where did you sit at the supper table?
7. What was the conversation like at the table?
8. Who was the "warm" person for you at the table?

---

9. What were the "happy times" at this table?
10. How did your family praise you? And for what?
11. Who did you look up to at this table?
12. What was so special about this person?
13. How did your family deal with problems at this table?
14. If you could change one thing about this table, what would it be?
15. How has your childhood table affected the person you are today?
16. What would you like to keep from your childhood table for your children?

**Step Two: EMOTIONAL DIMENSION.** We like to think that rationality "makes the world go 'round." In reality, emotion "makes the world go 'round." We elect our presidents more on how we feel about them than we do on their policies. The reactions of Wall Street are based more on how traders and investors "feel" about the stock market than they are on the objective health of corporations. Marriages succeed or fail more on how spouses feel about one another than on making the relationship better through mutual give-and-take.

Emotions play an important part in our experience of wholeness. Yet many people never learn to express, understand, or use emotions in healthy ways. These shortcomings interfere with virtually every human relationship.

In this session, you will encounter the word *shalom* or peace. As stated in the first session, *shalom* is a Hebrew word that means inner peace, tranquility, harmony, health, and well-being. It is an all-encompassing word that refers to the Sabbath rest of God's creation, the cessation of all conflict, the restoration of God's purpose in creation, the return of the land to fruit-bearing, the reconciliation of humanity with God, man with man, man with nature, and man with himself. *Shalom* is the center of our well-being. While peace is a gift from God, we have to apply it to the various areas of our lives. We have been created for *shalom* in each dimension of our lives:

- ☐ spiritual
- ☐ physical
- ☐ vocational
- ☐ emotional
- ☐ relational
- ☐ volitional

**LEADER:** Choose the Option One Bible Study (below) or the Option Two Study (page 42).

In the Option One Study (from the Gospel of John), Jesus is with his disciples again, for the first time since the crucifixion. And in the Option Two Study, Paul writes to the Colossians about making Christ's peace a part of their daily lives.

**OPTION 1**

# 📖 BIBLE STUDY/30 Minutes/Groups of 4

*Leader: Help the group decide on Option One or Option Two for their Bible Study. Remember to divide into groups of four if there are more than seven. Ask one person in each group to be the Convener. Remind the Convener to move the group along so the Bible Study can be completed in 30 minutes.*

# Gospel Study/Shalom
## John 20:19–23

**STUDY**

Read John 20:19–23 and discuss your responses to the following questions with your group. Remember, Jesus has just done the impossible—he has risen from the dead! Drop in on his followers and try to figure out what is wrong—and what Jesus did to turn things around. Remember, the word "peace" is the Hebrew word *shalom*.

> *¹⁹ On the evening of that first day of the week, when the disciples were together, with the doors locked for fear of the Jews, Jesus came and stood among them and said, "Peace be with you!" ²⁰ After he said this, he showed them his hands and side. The disciples were overjoyed when they saw the Lord.*
> *²¹ Again Jesus said, "Peace be with you! As the Father has sent me, I am sending you." ²² And with that he breathed on them and said, "Receive the Holy Spirit. ²³ If you forgive anyone his sins, they are forgiven; if you do not forgive them, they are not forgiven."*
>
> *John 20:19–23, NIV*

1. If you had been a reporter for *The Jerusalem Herald*, what headline would you have used to report this event?
   ❑ "Poltergeist Appears at Religious Gathering!"
   ❑ "He's BA-ACK!"
   ❑ "Christian Gathering Turns SPIRITED!"
   ❑ "Resurrected Prophet Gives Disciples 'Peace Sign'!"
   ❑ "Disciples Stunned—Jesus Returns Like He Said He Would!"

2. It's Easter morning. Jesus has broken the chains of death. And his disciples are behind locked doors. Why?
   ❑ They didn't believe what Jesus said he would do.
   ❑ They were afraid for their lives.
   ❑ They just wanted to be alone.
   ❑ They liked small groups.

3. Suddenly, Jesus steps into the room. In sports language, what does he do?
   ❑ He tears them up.
   ❑ He does a little reality therapy.
   ❑ He gives them new hope.
   ❑ He shows them a new game plan.
   ❑ He lets them stew in their own pain.

*"The man who screams at a football game but is distressed when he hears of a sinner weeping at the cross and murmurs about the dangers of emotionalism, hardly merits intelligent respect."*
—W. E. Sangster

**4.** This word "peace" is the Greek word for *shalom*—or complete harmony (spiritually, emotionally, and in every way). What do you think this word meant to the disciples at that moment in their lives?
   ❐ The "game" was not yet over.
   ❐ God had not disowned them because they ran away and hid.
   ❐ It was okay to feel down, but there was a new day ahead.
   ❐ It probably didn't mean much to them.

**5.** How would you compare your life right now to the disciples?
   ❐ Emotionally, I am "in hiding."
   ❐ I've put locks on the door of my life to protect me from people.
   ❐ I'm in a "cocoon" when I should be reaching out.
   ❐ I'm spending a lot of time with my most supportive friends.
   ❐ I'm like them after Jesus came—full of joy!
   ❐ I'm like them after Jesus came—I feel sent on a mission.
   ❐ I'm not like them at all.

**6.** Emotionally, if you had to graph the last six months of your life, what would the graph look like?

| High | |
|---|---|
| | |
| Low | |

Month  1      2      3      4      5      6

**7.** What are you most likely to hide from?
   ❐ the pain of my past
   ❐ people who might not accept me
   ❐ responsibility for my actions
   ❐ pressure!!!
   ❐ the demands of God
   ❐ anyone trying to give me a job
   ❐ facing who I really am
   ❐ the troubles of the modern world

41

**LEADER: When you have completed the Bible Study, move on to the Caring Time (page 44).**

**8.** In the midst of hiding, what would happen if Jesus stepped into your life today and said "*shalom*"—be at peace with yourself?

**9.** What do you need to do to receive the promised power of the Holy Spirit, and come out of hiding?
☐ know more about who (or what) the Holy Spirit is
☐ believe that I don't have to do it all on my own
☐ believe that the Holy Spirit truly is available to me
☐ pray for it
☐ I don't have a clue.

**OPTION 2**

# Epistle Study/Road to Recovery
## Colossians 3:1–4, 15–17

**STUDY**

Take a moment to reflect on the words of the Apostle Paul to the church in Colossae on the "practice of peace." Read Colossians 3:1–4, 15–17 and use the questions below to discuss how this works.

**3** *Since, then, you have been raised with Christ, set your hearts on things above, where Christ is seated at the right hand of God. ²Set your minds on things above, not on earthly things. ³For you died, and your life is now hidden with Christ in God. ⁴When Christ, who is your life, appears, then you also will appear with him in glory.*

*¹⁵Let the peace of Christ rule in your hearts, since as members of one body you were called to peace. And be thankful. ¹⁶Let the word of Christ dwell in you richly as you teach and admonish one another with all wisdom, and as you sing psalms, hymns and spiritual songs with gratitude in your hearts to God. ¹⁷And whatever you do, whether in word or deed, do it all in the name of the Lord Jesus, giving thanks to God the Father through him.*

*Colossians 3:1–4, 15–17, NIV*

**1.** Who does the Apostle Paul sound like in this passage?
☐ my old high school coach
☐ an army sergeant at boot camp
☐ a radio preacher
☐ the lecturer of the Dale Carnegie Institute
☐ my psychologist
☐ nobody I know
☐ other: _____

2. Which of these actions, mentioned in this passage, do you think helps a person to find the peace also promised here?
   ☐ setting our minds on things above, not on transient earthly things (vv. 1–2)
   ☐ dying to self and learning to live for others (v. 3)
   ☐ being thankful for what we have (v. 15)
   ☐ keeping in touch with the word of Christ through Bible reading (v. 16)
   ☐ praising God in song (v. 16)

3. If you could point to a time in your life when you were most at peace with yourself and with God, which period of your life would that be?
   ☐ right now
   ☐ when life was not so complicated
   ☐ right after I became a Christian
   ☐ I don't remember ever really experiencing this.

4. What are some of the "earthly things" you focus on so much that it takes away your peace?
   ☐ financial stresses            ☐ what others think of me
   ☐ having what others have    ☐ world turmoil
   ☐ politics                          ☐ other: _____

5. What "things above" would you like to focus on more?
   ☐ God's promise of victory over death
   ☐ God's way of living through love and self-giving
   ☐ the fellowship in Christ that spans all times and all cultures
   ☐ the kingdom where people—not things—matter most
   ☐ being in communion with my Creator (and through my Creator, with all of life)
   ☐ other: _____

6. In which dimension of life do you need to experience God's peace—right now?
   ☐ spiritual: at-one-ment with God
   ☐ physical: the temple of God
   ☐ vocational: finding the music at work
   ☐ emotional: harmony
   ☐ relational: members one of another
   ☐ volitional: taking charge of my world

**LEADER: When you have completed the Bible Study, move on to the Caring Time (below).**

**7.** What next step do you need to take to experience this peace?
- ❐ change my focus away from earthly things, specifically ...
- ❐ be more thankful
- ❐ sing more songs of faith
- ❐ "die to myself" and find more ways to serve others
- ❐ make more time for Bible Study
- ❐ just relax and open my life to God's presence

**COMMENT**

There is no peace available on this earth which can compare to the peace that comes from God through Christ. All our striving and struggling is for nothing, if we don't accept God's free gift first.

Christ wants to work with us as we struggle in our everyday world to sense his peace in every area of our lives. As with all real-life issues in the Christian faith, Christ is there with us in our struggles and provides us encouragement and direction.

## ♡ CARING TIME/20 Minutes/All Together

*Leader: Bring all of the foursomes back together for a time of caring. Follow the three steps below.*

**SHARING**

**SELF-EXAMINATION.** Go back over the list of symptoms (see page 27) and put an "✗" by those that would be particularly true of you right now. Don't be too hard on yourself, but don't be too easy either.

**PRESCRIPTIONS:** If you had to write a prescription for yourself, what would you write? Check two on the list below and add one more for your spiritual life at the bottom. Then share with the group which prescriptions you have written for yourself. Share this as a prayer request.

*Recent medical research has found that a person's emotional health (or, more accurately, the lack of emotional health) can directly affect the body's immune system.*

℞ ❐ IF LONELY: Hug 3 people per day (or as needed).

℞ ❐ IF TIRED: Afternoon nap; no *David Letterman* for 3 weeks.

℞ ❐ IF LETHARGIC: Walk 3 miles per week; stop and smell the roses.

℞ ❐ IF DEPRESSED: Visit an old friend; reminisce about the good old days. Read a good book and take yourself out to dinner.

℞ ❐ IF OVERLOADED: Take 1 day off to reorder priorities; cut back on your schedule and spend 3 nights at home each week.

℞ ❐ IF OVERSTRESSED: Take Vitamin B complex; drink fresh orange juice; jog 1 mile per day (or walk briskly).

R℞ ☐ IF OVERWEIGHT: Cut back on sugar, white flour, and all snacks; do 3 push-ups daily—away from the table.

℞ ☐ IF BORED: Volunteer some time to the hospital, Little League, or local nursing home. Find someone who needs you.

℞ ☐ IF HYPERACTIVE: Run around the block until your socks stink. Volunteer your time at a preschool for a month.

℞ ☐ IF INSECURE: Talk to your pastor—he/she probably is too.

℞ ☐ IF BUMMED OUT: Take a walk around the park; admire the flowers and speak to people about the weather.

℞ ☐ IF FRUSTRATED: Enroll in an aerobic dancing class and sweat it out.

℞ ☐ IF_____: _____.

**PRAYER**

Remembering the requests which were just shared, close with a prayer time. The Leader can start a conversational prayer (short phrases and sentences), followed by group members. After an appropriate amount of time, the Leader can close the time of prayer by praying for any requests which were not mentioned.

**ACTION**

Plan two or three concrete steps you can take this week to help you fill out your prescription. For example: "If Depressed": "I will visit an old friend or treat myself to something special," or "If Bummed Out": "I will go for a long walk and stop and chat with a few people on the way."

# SESSION 6
# Relational Dimension

**PURPOSE:** To discover ways to improve our relationship with God and with others.

**AGENDA:**  Gathering    📖 Bible Study    ♡ Caring Time

OPEN

## ☕ GATHERING/10 Minutes/All Together

*Leader: Read the instructions for Step One and go first. Then read the Introduction and explain the choices for Bible Study.*

**Step One: CHOOSING PARTNERS.** Before you get into the Bible Study about relationships, take a moment to choose a partner from your group for each of the following situations. You can use a name only once. Read the first situation and have everyone call out the partner they would choose. Then go on to the next category.

- ❑ endurance dancing contest at the Astrodome
- ❑ scuba diving in the Caribbean with the Jacques Cousteau crew
- ❑ Monday night football color announcer with me
- ❑ executor of my estate
- ❑ astronaut to fly the space shuttle while I walk in space
- ❑ my bodyguard in the event I strike it rich
- ❑ Sancho for the next "windmill" I decide to chase
- ❑ space shuttle flight to Mars
- ❑ best man/maid of honor at my wedding
- ❑ trapeze act for the Barnum & Bailey Circus
- ❑ hot tub demonstration for *The Home Show*
- ❑ hang gliding off the Palisades
- ❑ author of my biography
- ❑ tag-team partner for a professional wrestling match

**Step Two: RELATIONAL DIMENSION.** We have considered the spiritual, physical, vocational, and emotional dimensions of wholeness. But it is the relational dimension which ties all of these elements together. It is our relationships with God, with ourselves, and with others which make our lives whole. Without relationships, life would not only be uninteresting, it would also be dehumanizing. Through our relationships, we learn what it means to be a human being.

But relationships in and of themselves are not good. Successful relationships with God and others take work in order to be healthy. They do not just happen. At the center of all successful relationships is love and respect. Healthy relationships are marked by equality— equal giving and receiving—or else you will find yourself in a co-dependent relationship. Healthy relationships are balanced ones and they add to our lives. Unhealthy relationships throw our lives off-balance—in all of the other areas.

**LEADER: Choose the Option One Bible Study (below) or the Option Two Study (page 50).**

In the Option One Study (from Matthew's Gospel), Jesus puts the responsibility for keeping good relationships on us. While it is easy enough to love those who love us, Jesus' standard is higher: we should love our enemies. In the classic passage of 1 Corinthians 13 (the Option Two Study), we see the inspiring example of Christ's love. We are challenged to love as he loved.

**OPTION 1**

 BIBLE STUDY/30 Minutes/Groups of 4

*Leader: Help the group choose an option for study. Divide into groups of four for discussion. Remind the Convener for each foursome to move the group along so the Bible Study can be completed in the time allotted. Have everyone return together for the Caring Time for the final 20 minutes.*

## Gospel Study/First Things First
## Matthew 5:21–26, 43–48

**STUDY**

Read Matthew 5:21–26, 43–48 and discuss your responses to the following questions with your group. This passage is part of Jesus' teaching known as the Sermon on the Mount.

*21 "You have heard that it was said to the people long ago, 'Do not murder, and anyone who murders will be subject to judgment.' 22 But I tell you that anyone who is angry with his brother will be subject to judgment. Again, anyone who says to his brother, 'Raca,' is answerable to the Sanhedrin. But anyone who says, 'You fool!' will be in danger of the fire of hell.*

*23 "Therefore, if you are offering your gift at the altar and there remember that your brother has something against you, 24 leave your gift there in front of the altar. First go and be reconciled to your brother; then come and offer your gift.*

*25 "Settle matters quickly with your adversary who is taking you to court. Do it while you are still with him on the way, or he may hand you over to the judge, and the judge may hand you over to the officer, and you may be thrown into prison. 26 I tell you the truth, you will not get out until you have paid the last penny.*

*43 "You have heard that it was said, 'Love your neighbor and hate your enemy.' 44 But I tell you: Love your enemies and pray for those who persecute you, 45 that you may be sons of your Father in heaven. He causes his sun to rise on the evil and the good, and sends rain on the righteous and the unrighteous. 46 If you love those who love you, what reward will you get? Are not even the tax collectors doing that? 47 And if you greet only your brothers, what are you doing more than others? Do not even pagans do that? 48 Be perfect, therefore, as your heavenly Father is perfect."*

*Matthew 5:21–26, 43–48, NIV*

1. If you had just heard this advice on relationships for the first time and did not know who had given it, what would be your first reaction?
   ❏ I believe in being nice, but there's no need to be a fanatic about it!
   ❏ This would cut out half of our communication in our family!
   ❏ It's a nice standard, but who could ever reach it?
   ❏ This could turn our world around.
   ❏ other: _____

2. Which of these standards would you have the hardest time living up to?
   ❏ not calling people names
   ❏ always reconciling with my brothers and sisters before I worship
   ❏ settling conflicts quickly
   ❏ loving my enemies

3. Of these relationships, which is likely to cause a stress attack in you?
   - ❑ a visit from my mother-in-law
   - ❑ the boss calling me into his/her office
   - ❑ seven days of rain on a family vacation
   - ❑ a barking dog at my neighbor's house
   - ❑ one word of criticism from a parent
   - ❑ the cold shoulder treatment from my spouse
   - ❑ an overdrawn bank account—because of my spouse

4. If you could pat yourself on the back for making improvements in your relationships, what could you point to?
   - ❑ I don't blow my top as much.
   - ❑ I'm able to receive criticism without getting defensive.
   - ❑ I'm getting better with my temper.
   - ❑ I'm learning to say "I'm sorry."
   - ❑ other: _____

5. When you're angry, which relationship is the hardest for you to reconcile?
   - ❑ my spouse
   - ❑ my kids, especially my teenager(s)
   - ❑ my parents, because we don't communicate
   - ❑ my friends—especially very close friends
   - ❑ my professional peers
   - ❑ my enemies

6. The Scripture passage talks about leaving your gift at the altar and going to make peace with your brother. How well do you practice this?
   - ❑ I'm going to give myself an A+ on this.
   - ❑ B+ for trying.
   - ❑ It all depends who it is.
   - ❑ I'm never wrong.
   - ❑ other: _____

7. If you take this Scripture seriously, what will you do about some of the bad relationships (personal or professional) in your life?
   - ❏ Well, I separate my secular life from my church life.
   - ❏ You can't make it in business today and keep open relationships with some people.
   - ❏ I can't do anything about the way some people have treated me.
   - ❏ Yes—I will need to make a few changes.
   - ❏ Why did you have to bring this up?

8. Which of these "enemies" would you have a hard time loving?
   - ❏ anyone from the IRS!
   - ❏ my ex-spouse
   - ❏ my spouse's ex-spouse
   - ❏ a rival at work
   - ❏ "conservatives"/"liberals" (whichever you are not!)
   - ❏ persons of a different race
   - ❏ those I fought in war
   - ❏ other: _____

LEADER: When you have completed the Bible Study, move on to the Caring Time (page 54).

9. When you leave this session today, how will you respond to the radical demands of this passage?
   - ❏ conveniently forget it, like I've always done before
   - ❏ struggle with it for weeks, but stay with the same relational patterns in the end
   - ❏ make some changes, but perhaps not all that this demands
   - ❏ shoot for it all—turn my life around with love!

OPTION 2

# Epistle Study/How's Your Love Life?
## 1 Corinthians 13:1–7

STUDY

Read 1 Corinthians 13:1–7 and share your responses to the following questions with your group. This passage (often called "the love chapter") is Paul's attempt to show "a more excellent way" of caring for others.

**13** If I speak in the tongues of men and of angels, but have not love, I am only a resounding gong or a clanging cymbal. [2] If I have the gift of prophecy and can fathom all mysteries and all knowledge, and if I have a faith that can move mountains, but have not love, I am nothing. [3] If I give all I possess to the poor and surrender my body to the flames, but have not love, I gain nothing.

[4] Love is patient, love is kind. It does not envy, it does not boast, it is not proud. [5] It is not rude, it is not self-seeking, it is not easily angered, it keeps no record of wrongs. [6] Love does not delight in evil but rejoices with the truth. [7] It always protects, always trusts, always hopes, always perseveres.

*1 Corinthians 13:1–7, NIV*

1. If you could summarize what Paul says here about love, what would it be?
   - ❏ Love is... *impossible*!
   - ❏ Love should be our highest value.
   - ❏ Love is being like Christ.
   - ❏ If you don't love somebody, you're nobody.
   - ❏ Other: _____

2. Which of the following advertising slogans for love would you pick, based on this chapter from Paul?
   - ❏ Love—All the best people are doing it!
   - ❏ Rattling around the old apartment feeling like a nobody?— Try Love!
   - ❏ Love—now 100% longer-lasting!
   - ❏ Love—it will take you to the next level!
   - ❏ Want to give the gift that keeps on giving?—Try Love!

3. Who in your life defined love for you by the way he or she lived?

4. As you seek to apply this passage to your life, how do you view it?
   - ❏ It's naively idealistic.
   - ❏ It's beautiful, but unlike any real-life love I have seen.
   - ❏ It's a standard that makes me all too aware of my own shortcomings.
   - ❏ It's a standard that will force me to reach for the best that is in me.
   - ❏ It's a standard that I am pretty close to reaching right now.
   - ❏ It's a standard which I will definitely need Christ's help in reaching.

*"We are born helpless. As soon as we are fully conscious we scover loneliness. We need others physically, emotionally, intellectually; we need them if we are o know anything, even ourselves."*
*—C. S. Lewis*

**5.** How would you rate yourself from 1 to 10 (1 being I NEED HELP HERE and 10 being I'M PRETTY GOOD) in each area of this Scripture passage? Circle a number for each item. Then share your scores.

*Love is patient:* I don't take out my frustrations on those I love. I am calm under pressure and careful with my tongue.
I NEED HELP HERE  1   2   3   4   5   6   7   8   9   10   I'M PRETTY GOOD

*Love is kind:* I think before I act, especially with those I love. I cushion anything I say with prayer and consideration.
I NEED HELP HERE  1   2   3   4   5   6   7   8   9   10   I'M PRETTY GOOD

*Love does not envy:* I am not jealous of my time when those I love need me or want me to do something special.
I NEED HELP HERE  1   2   3   4   5   6   7   8   9   10   I'M PRETTY GOOD

*Love does not boast:* I don't consider my role any more important than those I love—I don't talk like "I know better."
I NEED HELP HERE  1   2   3   4   5   6   7   8   9   10   I'M PRETTY GOOD

*Love is not proud:* I don't think of myself as better because I am better organized than those I love (or better at sports, or singing, or handling money).
I NEED HELP HERE  1   2   3   4   5   6   7   8   9   10   I'M PRETTY GOOD

*Love is not rude:* I don't make cutting or crude remarks when I don't get my way—I don't become silent and withdraw.
I NEED HELP HERE  1   2   3   4   5   6   7   8   9   10   I'M PRETTY GOOD

*Love is not self-seeking:* I don't put myself first. I try to think of those I love for spiritual and emotional support.
I NEED HELP HERE  1   2   3   4   5   6   7   8   9   10   I'M PRETTY GOOD

*Love is not easily angered:* I don't let little things bother me, especially with those I love. I have a muffler on my mouth.
I NEED HELP HERE  1   2   3   4   5   6   7   8   9   10   I'M PRETTY GOOD

*Love keeps no record of wrongs:* I don't keep score of the number of times those I love have said something or done something that upset me, and I don't bring it up when we have a disagreement.
I NEED HELP HERE  1   2   3   4   5   6   7   8   9   10   I'M PRETTY GOOD

*Love does not delight in evil:* I don't secretly rejoice when those I love get a speeding ticket (or get fat from eating too much, or win the lottery and then lose it in a poker game).

I NEED HELP HERE   1   2   3   4   5   6   7   8   9   10   I'M PRETTY GOOD

*Love rejoices in the truth:* I am filled with joy when I think that God is working out his perfect plan for those I love—to make these people fully mature in Christ one day.

I NEED HELP HERE   1   2   3   4   5   6   7   8   9   10   I'M PRETTY GOOD

*Love always protects:* I am always there for those I love—even when they upset me—seeking to comfort and care as Christ would.

I NEED HELP HERE   1   2   3   4   5   6   7   8   9   10   I'M PRETTY GOOD

*Love always trusts:* I believe in those I love and I believe in God. And I am willing to let God do the shaping and molding.

I NEED HELP HERE   1   2   3   4   5   6   7   8   9   10   I'M PRETTY GOOD

*Love always hopes:* I affirm the work that God is doing in those I love, and I am confident that God is able to bring his work in them to completion.

I NEED HELP HERE   1   2   3   4   5   6   7   8   9   10   I'M PRETTY GOOD

*Love always perseveres:* I am committed to the vows that I made to those I love, and I am prepared to see it through to the end.

I NEED HELP HERE   1   2   3   4   5   6   7   8   9   10   I'M PRETTY GOOD

6. Which relationship do you need to apply these teachings to right now?
   - ❑ my spouse
   - ❑ my children
   - ❑ my neighbors
   - ❑ my ex-spouse
   - ❑ my parents
   - ❑ a person I know at work
   - ❑ some people in my church
   - ❑ other: _____

**LEADER: When you have completed the ⸺ble Study, move on to the Caring Time (page 54).**

7. How would your emotions be affected if you tried to live up to this standard of love?
   - ❑ It would make me a nervous wreck!—I couldn't do it.
   - ❑ It would depress me (because of my failures).
   - ❑ It would excite me (because of the challenge).
   - ❑ It would revive me (because loving makes me feel good, too).
   - ❑ It would heal me (because loving people receive love back).
   - ❑ other: _____

#  CARING TIME/20 Minutes/All Together

*Leader: Bring all of the foursomes back together for a time of caring. Follow the three steps below.*

**SHARING**

**EVERYDAY BLESSINGS.** Ask everyone in the group to think about the person on their left. Choose an everyday object that reminds you of a special quality possessed by that person. You might choose a lightbulb (because that person lights up the room), or a stapler (because he/she holds the group together). Use one of the examples shown below, or come up with your own ideas:

When everyone is ready, tell your person what you selected and why it reminds you of them.

**PRAYER**

Share your prayer requests and close with a prayer time. The Leader can start a conversational prayer (short phrases and sentences), followed by group members. After an appropriate amount of time, the Leader can close the time of prayer by praying for any requests which were not mentioned.

**ACTION**

Plan two or three concrete steps you can take this week to develop your relationship with God and one other person.

# SESSION 7
# Volitional Dimension

**PURPOSE:**   To turn over the throne room in my life to Jesus Christ, and to decide about the next step for this group.

**AGENDA:**    Gathering   📖 Bible Study   ♡ Caring Time

OPEN

## ☕ GATHERING/10 Minutes/All Together

*Leader: This is the final session together. You may want to have your Caring Time first. If not, be sure to allow a full 25 minutes at the end of the session. Read the instructions for Step One and set the pace by going first. Then read the Introduction and move on to the Bible Study.*

**Step One: YOU REMIND ME OF...** Write your name on a slip of paper and put it in a hat. Ask everyone in the group to select a name from the hat, but don't tell anyone whom you have chosen. Select a famous person that best describes the person you have chosen. When everyone is finished, mention the name of the famous person you selected, and see if the group can guess which group member you are describing.

❑ **Martin Luther King, Jr.:** You have the qualities of looking out for people who need love and dignity.

❑ **Alexander the Great:** Hats off to someone who seems to conquer everything you set out to accomplish!

❑ **Admiral Byrd:** You have an adventurous spirit as you explore places that others might hesitate to go.

❑ **Joan of Arc:** Your faith is evident in the way you live, and you are willing to make sacrifices for your beliefs, inspiring those who know you.

❑ **Lady Bird Johnson:** You live life with zest and leave a colorful, flowery trail behind you wherever you go!

❑ **Coco Chanel:** You are a living example of elegance, style, and creativity.

❑ **Mother Teresa:** You are a hard-working servant who has inspired many to live a life which is devoted to God.

□ **Jonas Salk:** You have a healing hand; everyone you touch seems to find health and wholeness.

□ **George Washington Carver:** You never seem to slow down! You have an inventive spirit that makes the most out of everything.

□ **J.D. Rockefeller:** Like a wealthy philanthropist, you make the world a better place with everything you set out to do.

**INTRODUCTION**

**Step Two: VOLITIONAL DIMENSION.** We have examined various dimensions of our lives—spiritual, physical, vocational, emotional, and relational. We have discussed and studied how Christ calls us to a certain way of life— a way which often conflicts with the ways of the world.

Now we are faced with a final decision—our volitional dimension. Volition is defined as "an act of willing, choosing, or deciding. A conscious choice; decision. The power or capability of choosing, the will." The biggest question we face is, "Who is in charge of my life?" Before we automatically answer, "God, of course!", let us be sure that is the case. Many people today say that is true, but upon closer examination of their lives, we see that it isn't.

What does it mean to say, "God is in charge of my life"? It means that we actively and unconditionally choose God to be in control of every aspect of who we are. We invite God to take the throne in our hearts and in our lives. Then we continue to yield ourselves to Christ's lordship on a daily basis. It's the difference between being a redeemed sinner (Christ as Savior) and a true follower or disciple of Jesus Christ (Christ as Lord).

**LEADER: Choose the Option One Bible Study (below) or the Option Two Study (page 60).**

We will ask ourselves one simple question in this final study: "What is the passion in my life?" In the Option One Study, Paul talks about what he really wanted out of life, and therefore pursued with a passion. Then in his letter to the Philippians (the Option Two Study), Paul tells them what his passion in life has been and continues to be.

**OPTION 1**

## 📖 BIBLE STUDY/25 Minutes/Groups of 4

*Leader: For this final session, divide into groups of four (if there are more than seven in your group). Help the groups choose their Bible Study. Remind the Conveners to end their Bible Study time five minutes earlier than usual to allow ample time for your final Caring Time—deciding what the group will do next.*

# Gospel Study/Holy, Wholly, Holey
## Acts 20:22–38

STUDY

Read Acts 20:22–38 and discuss your responses to the following questions with your group. This study will show you a man who knew what he wanted out of life and pursued it with a passion. You can decide for yourself if he was balanced or not.

*22 "And now, compelled by the Spirit, I am going to Jerusalem, not knowing what will happen to me there. 23 I only know that in every city the Holy Spirit warns me that prison and hardships are facing me. 24 However, I consider my life worth nothing to me, if only I may finish the race and complete the task the Lord Jesus has given me—the task of testifying to the gospel of God's grace.*

*25 "Now I know that none of you among whom I have gone about preaching the kingdom will ever see me again. 26 Therefore, I declare to you today that I am innocent of the blood of all men. 27 For I have not hesitated to proclaim to you the whole will of God. 28 Keep watch over yourselves and all the flock of which the Holy Spirit has made you overseers. Be shepherds of the church of God, which he bought with his own blood. 29 I know that after I leave, savage wolves will come in among you and will not spare the flock. 30 Even from your own number men will arise and distort the truth in order to draw away disciples after them. 31 So be on your guard! Remember that for three years I never stopped warning each of you night and day with tears.*

*32 "Now I commit you to God and to the word of his grace, which can build you up and give you an inheritance among all those who are sanctified. 33 I have not coveted anyone's silver or gold or clothing. 34 You yourselves know that these hands of mine have supplied my own needs and the needs of my companions. 35 In everything I did, I showed you that by this kind of hard work we must help the weak, remembering the words the Lord Jesus himself said: 'It is more blessed to give than to receive.'"*

*36 When he had said this, he knelt down with all of them and prayed. 37 They all wept as they embraced him and kissed him. 38 What grieved them most was his statement that they would never see his face again. Then they accompanied him to the ship.*

***Acts 20:22–38, NIV***

1. How would you describe Paul, based on what you see of him in this passage? (Choose three.)
   - ☐ focused
   - ☐ a martyr
   - ☐ bold
   - ☐ overly-independent
   - ☐ faithful
   - ☐ emotional
   - ☐ balanced, "together"
   - ☐ paranoid
   - ☐ self-sacrificing
   - ☐ fanatic
   - ☐ caring
   - ☐ a workaholic
   - ☐ expressive
   - ☐ spiritual

2. In the volitional side of his life—his passion, drive and motivation—would you say that the Apostle Paul was healthy?
   - ☐ Well, yes ...
   - ☐ He probably drove a few people crazy, but he knew what he wanted to do and he did it.
   - ☐ I'm not sure he would be seen as a model for a healthy person today.
   - ☐ Who cares—God turned him into a powerful person.
   - ☐ It was because he was not balanced that he was used by God.

3. What does it mean to you that Paul was "compelled by the Spirit"?
   - ☐ He was in a trance.
   - ☐ He wasn't responsible for his own actions.
   - ☐ He was a slave, doing what he was told.
   - ☐ He was completely focused on what he was doing, and was convinced it was the Spirit's leading.
   - ☐ He had a great passion for what he was doing.
   - ☐ other: _____

4. How would you describe the power of the force driving Paul in his life, in terms of the following energy sources? Using the same categories, how would you describe the driving force in your life?
   - ☐ a jet engine
   - ☐ a 450 hp V-8, with turbo-drive
   - ☐ a strong V-6 engine
   - ☐ a little 4-cylinder job
   - ☐ that battery on the back of the "Energizer bunny"
   - ☐ a single generic-brand AAA battery
   - ☐ a wind-up mechanical mainspring

5. Paul went to Jerusalem, "not knowing what would happen" to him there. When was the last time you made a major decision involving that much uncertainty?
   ❑ when I got married
   ❑ when I moved
   ❑ having/adopting a child
   ❑ I make risky decisions every day.
   ❑ every time I make a major purchase
   ❑ when I changed jobs
   ❑ when I accepted Christ
   ❑ Never!—I like certainty.

6. If you gathered all of the people you care about together, and you knew it would be the last time you would see them, what message would you want to give them?

7. If you knew you were going to die, which task or life objective (see verse 24) would be essential that you finish? What does that say about the passion of your life?

8. What would you like your desire or passion to be?
   ❑ I know I'm supposed to say "God," but I'm not there yet.
   ❑ I want it to be God, but I am pulled in so many other directions.
   ❑ allowing God to be in control of my life
   ❑ what my passion is now—God and his call on my life
   ❑ I'm not ready to answer that question.

9. How would you describe the communication channels between God and you right now—especially when it comes to knowing what God is calling you to do? Put an "*X*" on the line somewhere between the two extremes:

   _____

   **God is on the phone**          **I make sure the line**
   **right now**                          **is tied up**

10. After comparing your passion to Paul's, what is the "bottom line" for you in terms of where your life goes from here?
    ❑ I'm glad I'm more "low-key"—I just have fun!
    ❑ Paul and I have different styles—and I'm glad!
    ❑ I would like to have more of Paul's drive and passion.
    ❑ I need God to point me to a task I can feel strongly about.
    ❑ I'm pretty much like Paul right now—and it worries me!
    ❑ I'm pretty much like Paul now—and I'm glad!

LEADER: When you have completed the ble Study, move on to the Caring Time (page 62).

# Epistle Study/One Passion
## Philippians 3:4–14

Read Philippians 3:4–14 and discuss your responses to the following questions with your group. Here's your chance to compare the passion in your life to the passion of the Apostle Paul's life.

> *4 If anyone else thinks he has reasons to put confidence in the flesh, I have more: 5 circumcised on the eighth day, of the people of Israel, of the tribe of Benjamin, a Hebrew of Hebrews; in regard to the law, a Pharisee; 6 as for zeal, persecuting the church; as for legalistic righteousness, faultless.*
>
> *7 But whatever was to my profit I now consider loss for the sake of Christ. 8 What is more, I consider everything a loss compared to the surpassing greatness of knowing Christ Jesus my Lord, for whose sake I have lost all things. I consider them rubbish, that I may gain Christ 9 and be found in him, not having a righteousness of my own that comes from the law, but that which is through faith in Christ—the righteousness that comes from God and is by faith. 10 I want to know Christ and the power of his resurrection and the fellowship of sharing in his sufferings, becoming like him in his death, 11 and so, somehow, to attain to the resurrection from the dead.*
>
> *12 Not that I have already obtained all this, or have already been made perfect, but I press on to take hold of that for which Christ Jesus took hold of me. 13 Brothers, I do not consider myself yet to have taken hold of it. But one thing I do: Forgetting what is behind and straining toward what is ahead, 14 I press on toward the goal to win the prize for which God has called me heavenward in Christ Jesus.*
>
> *Philippians 3:4–14, NIV*

1. From what you see here, what is the "prize" that Paul seeks above all else—what motivates him? (Mark them 1, 2 and 3.)

   __ pride                    __ recognition

   __ eternal life            __ pleasing Christ

   __ finding acceptance      __ guilt

   __ group affiliation       __ perfectionism

   __ wholeness               __ fellowship

2. What does it mean when Paul says he is willing to consider all things as loss for Christ's sake?
   ❐ He thinks Christ wants him to be a monk and give up everything.
   ❐ Everything else is of much less value to him than pleasing Christ.
   ❐ He was ready to give up on all other ways to heaven.
   ❐ He wanted to show how totally focused he was on Christ.
   ❐ other: _____

3. Which of your skills and strengths do you have "reason to put confidence in"? "I have confidence in my..."
   ❐ ability to get along with people  ❐ parenting ability
   ❐ business and financial skills  ❐ ability to persuade people
   ❐ ability to listen  ❐ ability to cook a great dinner
   ❐ driving ability  ❐ biblical understanding
   ❐ my ability to teach others  ❐ other: _____

4. How would you compare your "spiritual beginnings" to Paul's?
   ❐ very similar—I was in all the "right" religious groups and activities.
   ❐ somewhat similar—I went to church and Sunday School most of the time.
   ❐ somewhat dissimilar—Church was there, but not a big part of my life.
   ❐ somewhat dissimilar—My spiritual background was not Jewish or Christian.
   ❐ very dissimilar—I once knew a kid who knew a kid who went to church!

5. How would you describe your spiritual "race" in athletic terms?
   ❐ I'm a little off my training routine—spiritually.
   ❐ I'm just now figuring out what this race is all about.
   ❐ I'm starting to catch my second wind.
   ❐ I'm sorry you asked.
   ❐ other: _____

**6.** What is the "prize" that you want in life, above all others?
- ❏ achievement and recognition
- ❏ wholeness
- ❏ love and acceptance
- ❏ a sense of connection to all of life
- ❏ eternal life
- ❏ raising my children right
- ❏ pleasing Christ
- ❏ just making it through without falling apart!
- ❏ other: _____

**7. SELF-EXAMINATION:** If you were to take charge of your life and truly seek to make Jesus Christ Lord in every area, what are some things that need to be changed? Below is a grocery list of things. Rank the top 5 you need to work on:

LEADER: When you have completed the Bible Study, move on to the Caring Time (below).

| | | | |
|---|---|---|---|
| _____ diet control | | _____ voting record | |
| _____ regular exercise | | _____ family responsibilities | |
| _____ financial planning | | _____ peer relationships | |
| _____ time management | | _____ TV viewing | |
| _____ community involvement | | _____ thought control | |
| _____ faith development | | _____ simple lifestyle | |
| _____ driving habits | | _____ workaholism | |
| _____ alcohol/smoking habit | | _____ laziness | |
| _____ proper sleep | | _____ tithing | |

## ♡ CARING TIME/25 Minutes/All Together

*Leader: This is decision time. These four steps are designed to help you evaluate your group experience and to decide about the future.*

**EVALUATION**

Take a few minutes to look back over your experience and reflect. Go around on each point and finish the sentences.

**1.** I have learned the following about whol-i-ness in my life from this series of Bible studies:

**2.** As I see it, our purpose and goal as a group was to:

**3.** We achieved our goal(s):
- ❏ completely
- ❏ almost completely
- ❏ somewhat
- ❏ We blew it.

**4.** The high point in this course for me has been:
- ❐ the Scripture exercises
- ❐ the sharing
- ❐ discovering myself
- ❐ belonging to a real community of love
- ❐ finding new life and purpose for my life
- ❐ the fun of the fellowship

**5.** One of the most significant things I learned was:

**6.** In my opinion, our group functioned:
- ❐ smoothly, and we grew
- ❐ pretty well, but we didn't grow
- ❐ it was tough, but we grew
- ❐ it was tough, and we didn't grow

**7.** The thing I appreciated most about the group as a whole is:

**ONTINUATION**

Do you want to continue as a group? If so, what do you need to improve? Finish the sentence:

*"If I were to suggest one thing we could work on as a group,
it would be ..."*

**MAKE A COVENANT**

A covenant is a promise made to each other in the presence of God. Its purpose is to indicate your intention to make yourselves available to one another for the fulfillment of the purposes you share in common. In a spirit of prayer, work your way through the following sentences, trying to reach an agreement on each statement pertaining to your ongoing life together. Write out your covenant like a contract, stating your purpose, goals, and the ground rules for your group. Then ask everyone to sign.

**1.** The purpose of our group will be ... (finish the sentence)

**2.** Our goals will be ...

**3.** We will meet for _____weeks, after which we will decide if we wish to continue as a group.

4. We will meet from \_\_\_\_\_ to _____ and we will strive to start on time and end on time.

5. We will meet at _____ (place) or we will rotate from house to house.

6. We will agree to the following ground rules for our group (check):

   ☐ **Priority**: While you are in the course, you give the group meetings priority.

   ☐ **Participation**: Everyone participates and no one dominates.

   ☐ **Respect**: Everyone is given the right to their own opinion, and "dumb questions" are encouraged and respected.

   ☐ **Confidentiality**: Anything that is said in the meeting is never repeated outside the meeting.

   ☐ **Empty Chair**: The group stays open to new people at every meeting, as long as they understand the ground rules.

   ☐ **Support**: Permission is given to call upon each other in time of need at any time.

   ☐ **Accountability**: We agree to let the members of the group hold us accountable to the commitments which each of us make in whatever loving ways we decide upon.

**CURRICULUM**

If you decide to continue as a group for a few more weeks, what are you going to use for study and discipline? There are 15 other studies available at this 201 Series level. 301 Courses, designed for deeper Bible Study with Study Notes, are also available.

For more information about small group resources and possible directions, please contact your small group coordinator or SERENDIPITY at 1-800-525-9563.